OXFORD REVISION GUI

A Level

Advanced

ECONOMICS

through diagrams

Andrew Gillespie

Oxford University Press

Oxford University Press, Great Clarendon Street, Oxford OX2 6DP

Oxford New York
Athens Auckland Bangkok Bogota
Buenos Aires Calcutta Cape Town Chennai Dar es Salaam
Delhi Florence Hong Kong Istanbul Karachi
Kuala Lumpur Madrid Melbourne Mexico City
Mumbai Nairobi Paris São Paulo Singapore
Taipei Tokyo Toronto Warsaw

and associated companies in
Berlin Ibadan

Oxford is a trade mark of Oxford University Press

First published 1998

ISBN 0 19 913287 9

Typesetting, design and illustration by Hardlines, Charlbury, Oxford
Printed in Great Britain

CONTENTS

Answering economics exam questions

What skills will you need? To do well in economics you must show that you know the theories, can explain them, can apply them to the given question, can analyse the implications of the theories or reasoning behind them, and show judgment in your answer. Remember it is not just about learning the material - you must relate it to the question set and discuss the validity of your arguments.

What to do when revising: Get hold of the syllabus. Break it down into manageable sections. Produce a revision timetable. Tick off items as you cover them. Summarise your notes into brief, memory jogging revision notes. Learn: What do the terms mean? What is the relationship between the different variables? What are the relevant diagrams? What is the significance of the topic - why have you studied it? Take 'investment', for example - What is it? What affects it? What are the consequences of it changing? Also, make sure you get hold of past papers - see how examiners have asked about topics in recent years. Practise!

In the exam room: Check you know exactly how much time you have, what you have to do, how many questions you must answer. Write down when you must move on to the next question. Quickly read through the whole paper a couple of times. Think before writing. Watch your time. Do not get carried way with the topics you know well and delay starting questions where you are more uncertain. Plan your answers to make sure you are answering the question properly.

Answering questions: Read the question. Read it again! One of the major mistakes that candidates make is that they fail to answer the question set. Once you get started on an answer it is very difficult to change it, so make sure you answer the question correctly first time. Read the question thoroughly, think about how you will answer it *before* you begin.

Look for the trigger words: Make sure you think about the type of question before answering. If the question asks you to 'identify' or 'describe' these are basic skills - you should simply make a series of points. If it asks you to 'explain' or 'account for' something you must show why these points are relevant. 'Analyse' or 'examine' means you should develop your argument in greater detail - What are the potential consequences of a particular change? Is there a secondary effect? Is the outcome certain? 'Consider', 'assess' or 'evaluate' means you need to weigh up the points you have made - Are they always true? What other factors are there? How reliable is the data? Do the facts fit the theory? Is the theory flawed? Are there alternative views? What is most likely to be the effect? Least likely? What does it depend on? Try to avoid simply listing points with these types of questions; discuss your ideas.

Look for specific words: check whether the question wants examples or refers to a specific situation, such as a 'dramatic', 'sudden', 'long term', or 'short term' change. Any extra words in the question need to be referred to in your answer.

Data response questions: Avoid general, journalistic answers. Make sure you have some economic theory! Try to explain your points with reference to economic analysis; illustrate your points with diagrams if you can. Avoid simply repeating the data, e.g. it goes up by 12%, down by 5%, down by 2%. Look for trends, overall changes and patterns within the trend, e.g. seasonal fluctuations or economic cycles. Think about causes and effects - What has brought about this pattern? What is the likely impact of the trends in the data? Relate your answer to theory.

Remember: to do well in high mark questions you must: show you know the topic, develop your points, relate them to the question and consider the significance/validity/underlying assumptions of your arguments. The depth of your argument is more important than making a series of points.

Avoid: i) answering too many or too few questions(!), believe it or not this is quite common; make sure you know what to do on each paper, **ii)** being too descriptive - develop your ideas, **iii)** answering the question you wished they had set instead of the one they did set.

Good luck!

Introduction to Economics

Types of economics

- **Positive economics** is based on testable theories, e.g. the idea that higher interest rates lead to a fall in aggregate demand can be tested by looking at past data.

- **Normative economics** is based on opinion, e.g. the idea that the Government should make the reduction of unemployment its priority, is one person's view; another person might think it is more important to increase growth. Normative statements often have 'should' or 'ought to' in them; they involve value judgements.

- **Microeconomics** focuses on individual markets and decisions by individual households and firms.

- **Macroeconomics** focuses on the economy as a whole, e.g. it considers the price level for the economy as a whole, rather than for one market.

Sectors of the economy

- **Private sector:** resources owned by private individuals
- **Public sector:** resources owned by the State
- **Primary sector:** extractive industries, e.g. forestry, fishing, coal
- **Secondary sector:** converts materials into goods, e.g. manufacturing
- **Tertiary sector:** service sector, e.g. finance, tourism

In the UK this century, the service sector has been growing and the primary sector has been declining.

Factors of production

- **Land:** natural resources, e.g. land itself, minerals, the sea
- **Labour:** human resources; this depends on the population size, the working age, people's skills and the level of training
- **Capital:** man-made aids to production, e.g. factories and equipment
- **Entrepreneurship:** this is the ability to combine factors of production and take risks in establishing new ventures

Types of production
- Capital intensive: uses relatively high amounts of capital compared to other factors of production, e.g. oil refining
- Labour intensive: uses relatively high amounts of labour compared to other factors of production, e.g. hairdressing

Scarcity and choice

At any moment in time output in an economy is limited by the resources and technology available. However, consumers' wants are unlimited and so decisions must be made about:

- What to produce? What goods and services should be made with the resources available?

- How to produce? What is the most efficient means of using the resources?

- For whom to produce? How are the goods and services allocated amongst consumers?

These are the three basic economic problems. Different economic systems solve them in different ways.

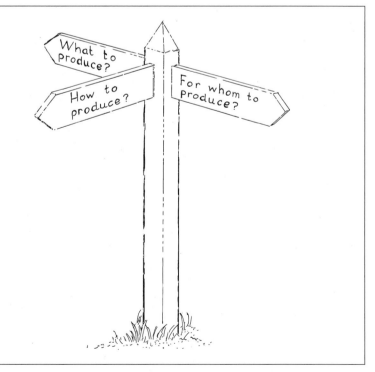

Introduction to Economics continued

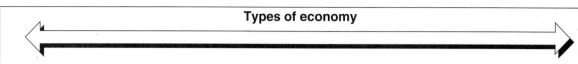

Types of economy

Free market: the allocation of resources is left to market forces of supply and demand.

Private sector

Mixed economy: some of the decisions are made by the Government and some are made by market forces.

Command or planned economy: the Government decides what is produced, how it is produced, and for whom.

Public sector

In reality, all economies are mixed to some degree, but vary in the extent to which the Government intervenes. In the 1980s and 1990s, the UK Government has been trying to reduce its involvement in the economy (e.g. through privatisation) and increase the role of the private sector. This trend has been followed in many other countries, e.g. the decline of Communism in Eastern Europe.

Opportunity cost is the sacrifice foregone in the next best alternative. If a firm invests more in project A rather than project B, for example, then project B is the opportunity cost. If we use our income to buy X not Y, Y is the opportunity cost.

Types of goods
- **Capital goods (producer goods):** used to produce consumption goods in the future, e.g. machinery and equipment; not bought for final consumption.
- **Consumption goods:** bought for final consumption, e.g. washing machines, videos. Consumer non-durables (e.g. food) are immediately consumed; consumer durables are not consumed immediately, e.g. televisions.
- **Free goods:** involve no opportunity cost, e.g. air. Note: nowadays <u>clean</u> air may have an opportunity cost because resources are needed to remove pollution.

Production Possibility Frontier (PPF) or Production Possibility Curve (PPC)
shows the maximum combination of goods and services which can be produced given the existing level of resources.

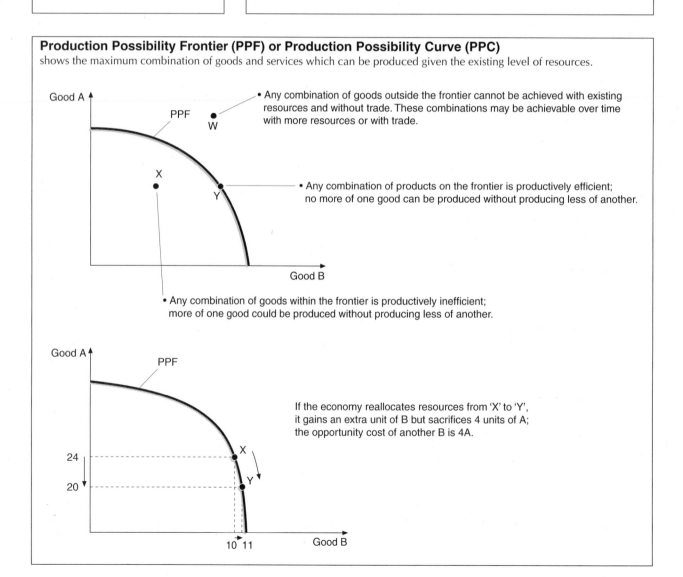

- Any combination of goods outside the frontier cannot be achieved with existing resources and without trade. These combinations may be achievable over time with more resources or with trade.

- Any combination of products on the frontier is productively efficient; no more of one good can be produced without producing less of another.

- Any combination of goods within the frontier is productively inefficient; more of one good could be produced without producing less of another.

If the economy reallocates resources from 'X' to 'Y', it gains an extra unit of B but sacrifices 4 units of A; the opportunity cost of another B is 4A.

Introduction to Economics continued

Shape of the production possibility frontier

usually convex to the origin due to the law of diminishing returns - as resources are transferred from Good A to Good B, the extra output of B becomes successively smaller, whilst the amount being sacrificed in A become successively larger.

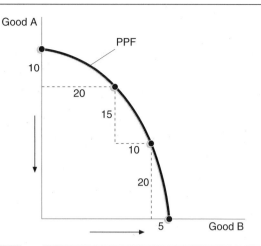

If returns are constant, the PPF is a straight line - as resources are transferred from one good to another, the amount of output sacrificed by one good and gained by the other is constant.

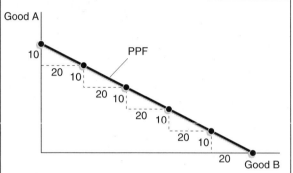

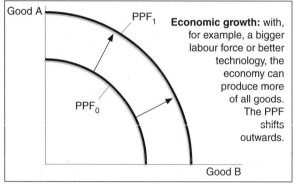

Economic growth: with, for example, a bigger labour force or better technology, the economy can produce more of all goods. The PPF shifts outwards.

Types of economy

Free Market

- decisions are made by individual buyers and sellers who act in their own self interest; producers aim to maximize their profits; consumers aim to maximize their utility
- the price mechanism allocates resources

Command or planned economy

- decisions made by central planning agency
- State ownership of resources
- prices set by the State
- motive for production is social welfare
- lack of market forces

Advantages of the free market
- resources are allocated by market forces and the price mechanism (called the Invisible Hand by Adam Smith); there is no Government intervention
- the profit motive provides an incentive to reduce costs and be innovative
- the free market maximizes community surplus if there are no failures and imperfections

Disadvantages of free market
see market failures and imperfections on pages 20–22
e.g.
- public goods
- merit goods
- externalities
- instability

Free Market

Advantages of the command or planned economy
- the Government can influence the distribution of income to make it more equal
- the Government can determine which goods are supplied (e.g. it can prevent the production of socially undesirable goods)

Command or Planned economy

Disadvantages of the command or planned economy
- requires an enormous amount of information (and almost inevitably there will be information overload leading to inefficiency); often bureaucratic
- no incentive for individuals or firms to be innovative; lack of a profit motive; goods are often poor quality and usually a limited choice
- liable to lead to allocative and productive inefficiency due to lack of competition and no profit motive

Demand

A demand curve shows the quantity that consumers are willing and able to purchase at each and every price, all other things unchanged. If other things do change (e.g. the consumers' incomes rise) the consumers are likely to want more or less at each and every price and the demand curve shifts.

The law of demand states that a higher quantity will be demanded at a lower price assuming all other factors remain constant.

The demand for a product or service depends on factors such as the price, consumers' income, the price of other goods, advertising, the consumers' tastes.

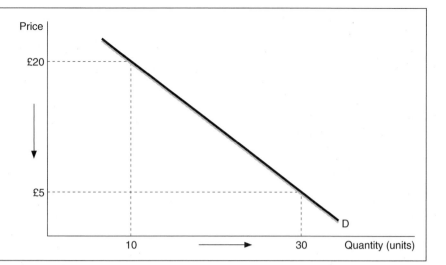

Movements along the demand curve: extensions and contractions

A change in the price will lead to a 'change in the quantity demanded'. This is shown by a movement along the demand curve.

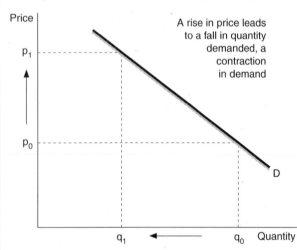

A rise in price leads to a fall in quantity demanded, a contraction in demand

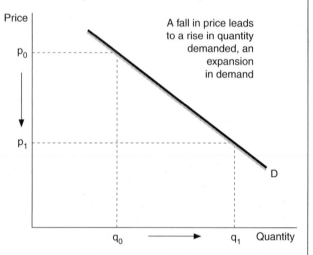

A fall in price leads to a rise in quantity demanded, an expansion in demand

Shift in demand

A change in any of the other factors affecting demand (except price) leads to a shift in demand. At each and every price there is an increase or decrease in the quantity demanded, so the demand curve shifts.

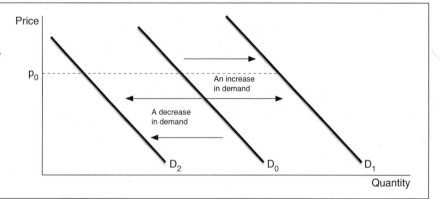

Outward shifts of the demand curve

The demand curve will shift outwards when more is demanded at each and every price. This could be because:

- real incomes have risen (assuming the good is normal)
- the price of a substitute product has gone up, e.g. higher prices for coffee might increase demand for tea
- the price of a complement product has gone down, e.g. a fall in the price of cars might increase demand for petrol

- the product has been advertised more effectively
- the population has grown so there are more consumers
- tastes have changed so more people want the product
- more credit is available so people can borrow more money

Demand continued

Downward sloping demand curves

The demand curve is downward sloping because of the law of diminishing marginal utility. Each extra unit of a good or service will eventually give less extra satisfaction (utility); therefore the consumer will only be willing to pay less for more goods.

Note: although the consumer gets less extra satisfaction from each additional unit, his or her total satisfaction is rising.

Market demand curve: the horizontal summation of individuals' demand curves.

The price, income, and cross elasticity of demand (also see pages 11–13)

- The size of the change in the quantity demanded following a price change depends on the price elasticity of demand.
- The increase or decrease in demand following a change in income depends on the income elasticity of demand.
- The increase or decrease in demand following a change in the price of other goods depends on the cross elasticity of demand.

Upward sloping demand curves

The demand curve can slope upwards. This means more is demanded when the price increases. This can occur with

- 'ostentatious goods' – people want to be seen buying more expensive goods. Also called Veblen goods.
- Giffen goods – these are very inferior goods and, when they become more expensive, consumers cannot afford any other products, so spend what money they have on these.

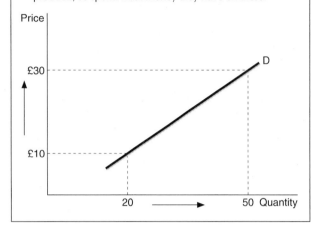

Income and substitution effects

If the price of a good falls, the quantity demanded will usually increase. This is because of:

- a substitution effect - with the fall in price of good A, A becomes relatively cheaper than other goods and inevitably there is a desire to buy more. Consumers inevitably switch to the relatively cheaper good.
- an income effect - with a lower price of good A, the consumer has more real income. If he/she bought the same amount of goods as before, there would be money left over. This means the consumer has more purchasing power because good A is cheaper. This leads to an income effect. If the good is normal, the consumers will want to buy more because of the income effect. This

means both the income and substitution effects make the consumer want to buy more.

If the good is inferior, the consumer will actually want to buy less; now that they have more real income they will want to switch away to buy more luxurious goods. The income effect therefore works against the substitution effect. However, the substitution effect is larger and so overall the consumers do buy more.

If the good is a Giffen good, the income effect again works against the substitution effect and actually outweighs it. This means that overall the quantity demanded falls when the price falls and so the demand curve is upward sloping.

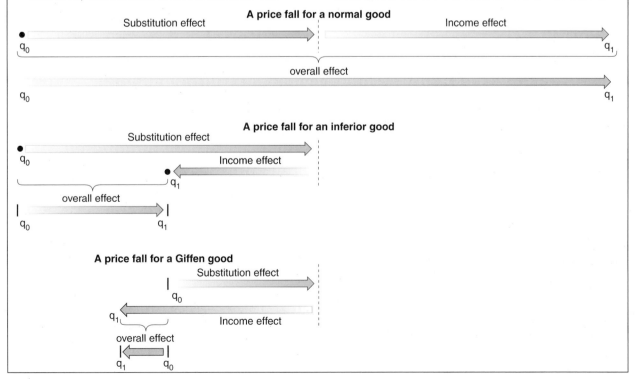

Demand continued

Utility
Utility is another word for satisfaction.

Marginal and total
Marginal utility (MU) is the extra satisfaction gained from consuming another unit of a good.
Total utility (TU) is the total satisfaction gained from consuming a given number of goods.

Law of diminishing marginal utility
states that successive units of consumption will eventually lead to a fall in their marginal utility.

Maximizing utility
We assume the aim of rational consumers is to maximize their utility, given the following constraints: a) limited income b) a given set of prices c) constant tastes.

To maximize utility, consumers will consume up to the point where

$$\frac{MU_A}{P_A} = \frac{MU_B}{P_B} = \frac{MU_C}{P_C} = \dots$$

This is known as the equi-marginal condition.

This means that the extra satisfaction per £ on the last unit of good A equals the extra satisfaction per £ on the last unit of good B and that of C and D and so on. If this was not the case, consumers would reorganize their spending and increase their satisfaction. For example, if the last A per £ was more satisfying than the last B; the consumer would buy more As and less Bs. (They could not have more of both as he or she is constrained by income.)

Paradox of value
Water is much more essential than diamonds but people are willing to pay more for diamonds. This is because there are relatively few of them and the marginal utility of another one is high. The total utility for them is quite low. However there is a large amount of water and so the extra utility of another unit is low. The total utility, however, is high.

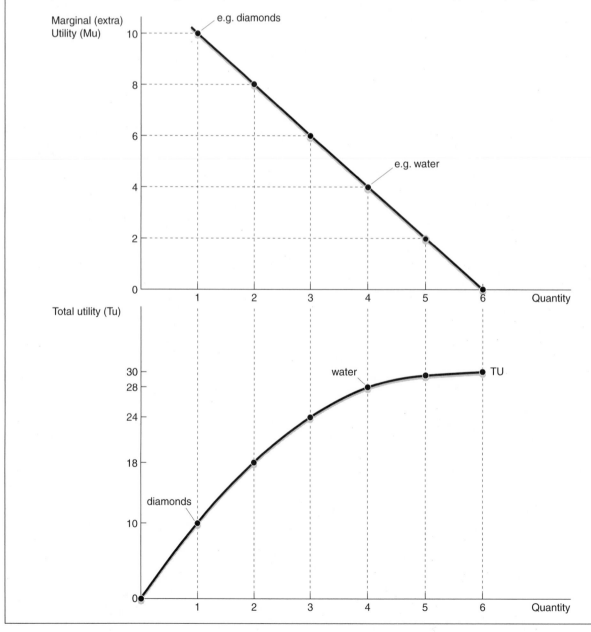

Elasticity of demand

The elasticity of demand measures the sensitivity of demand to a change in a variable. The variable might be the price of the good, the price of other goods, or income.

The sign of the answer depends on the direction in which the two parts of the equation move. If both demand and the variable move in the same direction (e.g. they both increase or both fall) the sign will be positive. If they move in different directions the answer will be negative, e.g. if demand rises when income rises, the answer will be positive; if demand falls when income rises, the answer will be negative.
The sign shows the direction of movement; it does not show the actual elasticity; this is shown by the size of the number (i.e. whether it is greater or less than one)

The size of the answer (ignoring the sign)
- If demand is elastic this means that the percentage change in demand is greater than the percentage change in the variable. The value of the answer (ignoring the sign) will be greater than one.
- If demand is inelastic this means that the percentage change in demand is less than the percentage change in the variable. The value of the answer (ignoring the sign) will be less than one.
- If demand is unit elastic the percentage change in demand is the same as the percentage change in the variable. The value of the answer (ignoring the sign) is equal to one.

Elasticity of demand

	Value	Description
Perfectly elastic	infinity	the percentage change in the quantity demanded is infinite
Elastic	>1	the percentage change in the quantity demanded is greater than the percentage change in the variable
Unit elastic	=1	the percentage change in the quantity demanded is equal to the percentage change in the variable
Inelastic	<1	the percentage change in the quantity demanded is less than the percentage change in the variable
Perfectly inelastic	0	there is no change in the quantity demanded

Price elasticity of demand
Measures the sensitivity of demand to a change in price.

$$\frac{\text{percentage change in quantity demanded}}{\text{percentage change in price}}$$

The sign
The price elasticity will usually be negative - when the price goes up, the quantity demanded falls, and vice versa. However, for a Giffen good or Veblen good, the price elasticity is positive. When price increases, the quantity demanded also rises.

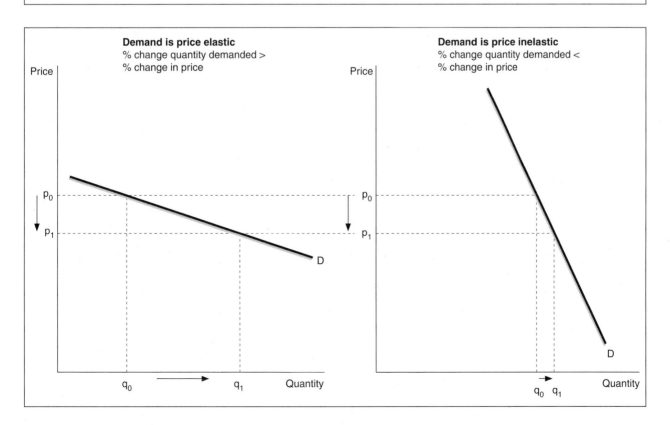

Demand is price elastic
% change quantity demanded >
% change in price

Demand is price inelastic
% change quantity demanded <
% change in price

Elasticity of demand continued

The size of the price elasticity of demand depends on
- the number and availability of substitutes. If there are many substitutes available, consumers can easily switch away if the firm increases its price. Demand will be more price elastic.
- the time horizon. In the short run it may not be easy to find alternatives and so demand is likely to be price inelastic. Over time, consumers can shop around and search for more substitutes and so demand is likely to be more price elastic.
- the percentage of income spent on the good, e.g. consumers only spend a small percentage of their income on salt and so are not very sensitive to price changes in this product. Demand is price inelastic. By comparison, washing machines, personal computers, and holidays take

a greater percentage of income and households are more likely to look around for the best price. These goods are more price sensitive.
- the type of good. Some goods are habit forming and so tend to be price inelastic. In the extreme case this could be drugs, but is also true of items such as newspapers and brands of coffee.
- the width of the definition. If we define the category of goods and services we are interested in very widely, demand will be more price inelastic, e.g. if we look at the demand for one brand of butter or margarine, consumers can switch easily to another brand if the price goes up; if we look at all brands, consumers are less likely to give up the product altogether.

Price elasticity and a straight line demand curve

Price elasticity will vary on a downward sloping straight line demand curve from being elastic on the top left, unit elastic in the middle and inelastic at the bottom right.

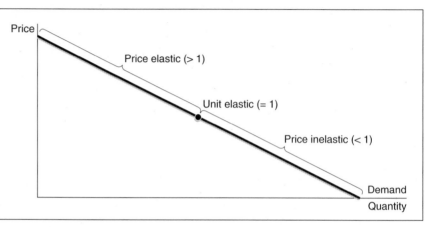

Extreme cases of price elasticity of demand

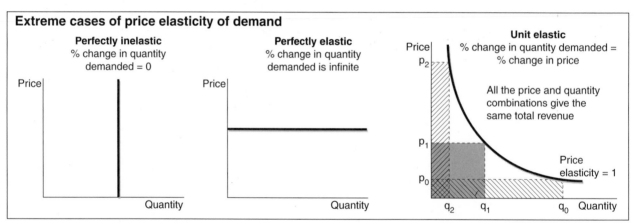

Price elasticity and revenue

If demand is price elastic, a fall in price will lead to an increase in revenue. Although each good is cheaper, the increase in the number demanded more than compensates for this and revenue increases overall.

If demand is price inelastic, a fall in price leads to a fall in revenue. The increase in the quantity demanded does not compensate for the fact that each unit is selling for less.

To increase revenue when demand is price inelastic, the firm should increase price.

If demand is unitary elastic the revenue does not change when price is changed.

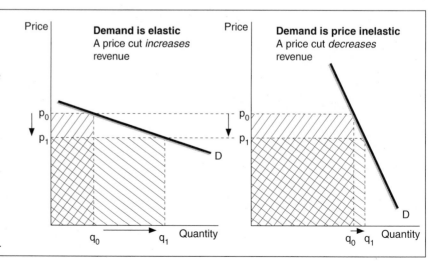

Elasticity of demand continued

Cross elasticity of demand

Measures the sensitivity of the demand for one good to a change in price of another.

Cross elasticity of good A with respect to good B =

$$\frac{\text{percentage change in quantity demanded of good A}}{\text{percentage change in the price of good B}}$$

If the two goods are substitutes, the cross elasticity will be positive. If good B increases in price, people switch to good A and demand for A rises.

If the goods are complements, such as golf clubs and golf balls, the sign will be negative. As the price of golf clubs rises, less people buy clubs and less people buy golf balls.

Income elasticity of demand

Measures the sensitivity of demand to a change in income.

$$\frac{\text{percentage change in the quantity demanded}}{\text{percentage change in income}}$$

The sign

If the good is normal, the income elasticity will be positive. As income rises, the quantity demanded rises. If the value is greater than 1, demand is income elastic, e.g. holidays abroad; these are often called 'luxuries', e.g. private health care. If the value is less than 1, demand is income inelastic, e.g. demand for bread; these are often 'necessities'.

If the good is inferior or Giffen, the income elasticity will be negative. With more income people switch from this good to a more superior good, e.g. they switch from supermarket branded products to a more exclusive brand name; from using buses to buying a car.

The size

The higher the figure (ignoring the sign), the greater the relationship between demand and income.

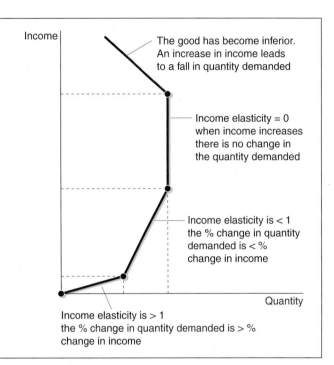

The good has become inferior. An increase in income leads to a fall in quantity demanded

Income elasticity = 0 when income increases there is no change in the quantity demanded

Income elasticity is < 1 the % change in quantity demanded is < % change in income

Income elasticity is > 1 the % change in quantity demanded is > % change in income

Types of goods

	Normal	Inferior	Giffen
Price elasticity	NEGATIVE If price rises, quantity demanded falls. Downward sloping demand curve	NEGATIVE If price rises, quantity demanded falls. Downward sloping demand curve	POSITIVE If price rises quantity demanded rises. Upward sloping demand curve
Income elasticity	POSITIVE When income rises quantity demanded increases	NEGATIVE When income rises quantity demanded falls as consumers switch to more luxurious products	NEGATIVE When income rises quantity demanded falls as consumers switch to more luxurious products

Uses of elasticity

Uses of price elasticity

- used to determine pricing policy - if demand is price inelastic, firms will increase price to raise revenue; if demand is price elastic firms will decrease price.
- firms can use it for planning, e.g. by estimating the effect of a price change, firms can plan the number of goods to produce, the number of people to employ, and the impact on cashflow.
- used when price discriminating to set price in each market.
- used by the Government to estimate the impact of an indirect tax increase in terms of sales and tax revenue.
- used to estimate the impact on consumer spending, producers' revenue, and income of any shift in supply.

Uses of cross elasticity

- firms can estimate the effect on their demand of a competitor's price cut.
- firms can estimate impact on demand for their product if they cut price of a complement, e.g. if they cut the price of the computer, how much will demand for software increase?

Uses of income elasticity

- can determine what goods to produce or stock, e.g. as the economy grows, firms might want to avoid inferior goods.
- can help firms plan production and employee requirements as the economy grows.
- can help firms estimate any potential changes in demand, e.g. as overseas incomes grow it may create new markets.

Supply

A supply curve shows the quantity that producers are willing and able to supply at each and every price, all other things unchanged.

According to the **law of supply** a higher quantity will be supplied at higher prices, all other things unchanged. The supply curve is derived from the marginal cost curve; as the extra cost of producing a unit increases, producers need a higher price to produce the product.

The supply of a product will depend on factors such as the number of producers, the state of technology, the prices of factors of production, indirect taxes and Government subsidies, and the aims of producers.

Movements along a supply curve: extensions and contractions

A change in the price of a good will lead to a change in the quantity supplied; this is shown as a movement along the supply curve.

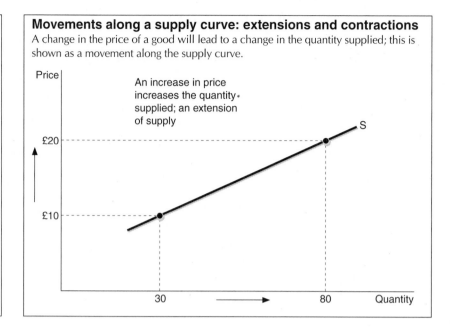

An increase in price increases the quantity supplied; an extension of supply

Shifts in supply

If other factors change (apart from the price) then more or less will be supplied at each and every price. This is shown as a shift in the supply curve or change in supply.

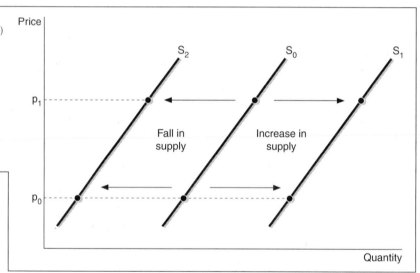

Fall in supply

Increase in supply

Outwards shifts in supply

If the supply curve shifts outwards, more is supplied at each and every price. This could be caused by:

- an increase in the number of suppliers
- an improvement in technology
- a fall in the prices of factors of production - if labour becomes cheaper, for example, more can be supplied at each price
- a cut in indirect tax or an increase in subsidies to producers
- a change in the prices of other goods, e.g. if good B falls in price, producers may switch their resources into good A, which will increase the supply of A. In some cases goods are supplied jointly, e.g. beef and hides. If a higher price leads to an increase in the quantity supplied of beef, this will also lead to the quantity of hides produced increasing at each price.
- Other factors, e.g. changes in the weather can increase the supply of agricultural products; better management can improve the productivity of the workforce.

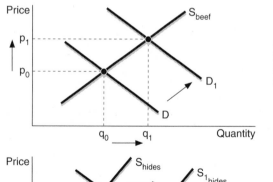

Beef market

An increase in demand for beef leads to more being supplied at a higher price

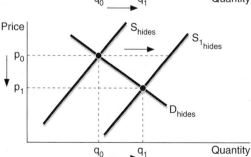

Hides market

An increase in the quantity of beef increases the supply of hides and leads to a fall in price

Supply continued

The price elasticity of supply

Measures the responsiveness of supply to a change in price.

$$\frac{\text{percentage change in the quantity supplied}}{\text{percentage change in the price}}$$

Size of answer (ignoring the sign)

- If the percentage change in supply is greater than the percentage change in price then supply is elastic. The answer will be bigger than one.
- If the percentage change in supply is less than the percentage change in price then supply is inelastic.

Any straight line supply curve:

- drawn from the origin has a unit price elasticity of supply.
- which would intersect with the price axis is price elastic
- which would intersect with the quantity axis is price inelastic

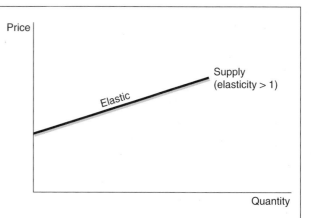

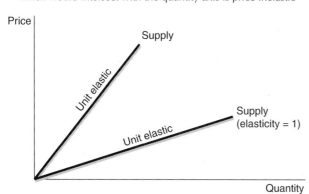

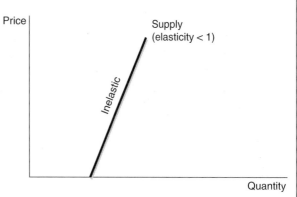

Extreme cases of the price elasticity of supply

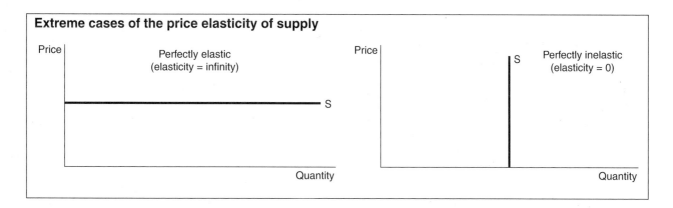

Determinants of the price elasticity of supply

- the number of producers. The more producers there are, the easier it should be for the industry to increase output in response to a price increase. Supply will be more elastic
- the existence of spare capacity. The more capacity there is in the industry, the easier it should be to increase output if price goes up. This makes supply more elastic.
- ease of storing stocks. If it is easy to stock goods, then if price rises the firm can sell these stocks and so supply is more elastic. In the case of goods such as fresh flowers, it may not be easy to store them and so supply will not be very flexible.
- the time period. Over time the firm can invest in training and more equipment and more firms can join the industry, so supply should be more flexible, i.e. more elastic.
- factor mobility, i.e. the easier it is for resources to move into the industry, the more elastic supply will be.
- length of the production period, i.e. the quicker a good is to produce, the easier it will be to respond to a change in price; supply in manufacturing is usually more price elastic than agriculture.

Periods of supply

- Momentary: supply totally inelastic
- Short run: constrained by fixed factors; supply usually inelastic
- Long run: all factors are variable, so supply is more elastic

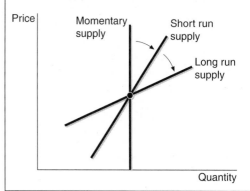

Demand and supply

In the market system, resources are allocated by the price mechanism. The price will adjust to equate supply and demand.

Equilibrium occurs when the quantity supplied equals the quantity demanded and there is no incentive for change, i.e. there is a state of rest.

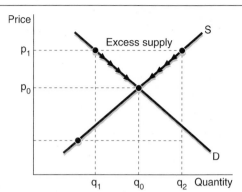

If the price is above the equilibrium price (e.g. p1) there will be excess supply (q1 q2); the quantity supplied is greater than the quantity demanded and the price will fall. As it does this, the quantity demanded will increase and the quantity supplied will fall. This will continue until the quantity supplied equals the quantity demanded and equilibrium is reached (p0q0).

If the price is below the equilibrium price, e.g. p3, there will be excess demand (q3q4); the quantity demanded will be greater than the quantity supplied. In this situation the price will rise. This will increase the quantity supplied and reduce the quantity demanded until equilibrium (p0q0).

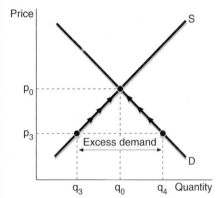

Condition	Description	Effect
quantity demanded > quantity supplied	excess demand/ shortage	price will rise
quantity demanded = quantity supplied	equilibrium	price remains the same
quantity demanded < quantity supplied	excess supply/ surplus	price will fall

The price mechanism
In the free market, the price acts as a rationing device, a signal, and incentive. If demand for a product increases, for example, this will lead to excess demand at the old price. The price will rise reducing the quantity demanded (rationing device), encouraging existing firms to produce more (incentive), and encouraging others to join the industry (signal). This brings resources into this industry and out of another.

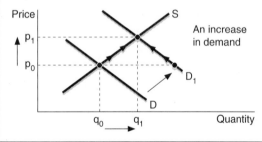

Price controls
A minimum price
This means that the price is not allowed to fall below a set level. If the market price is below this level the effect will be to create excess supply. For example, the Government has introduced a minimum wage rate. If this is set above the market rate, those who are still employed will earn more than before but there will be excess supply, i.e. the higher price will mean more people want to work but less are demanded.
Note: if the minimum price is below equilibrium it will have no effect.

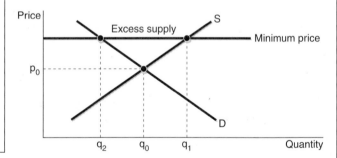

Maximum price
This sets a limit for the price, e.g. the Government might fix a maximum rent which can be charged. If the market price is above this level; the effect is to create excess demand.

Maximum prices often cause a black market to arise whereby people start trading at the market price rather than the 'official price', e.g. tickets for concerts are sometimes set lower than the market prices, which is why ticket touts buy them at the fixed price and sell them for more.
Note: if the maximum price is above equilibrium it will have no effect.

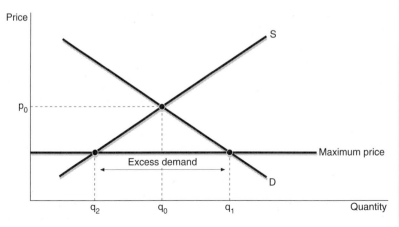

Demand and supply continued

Demand and supply issues

- *No equilibrium:* It may not be possible to supply a good because there is no equilibrium price

- *The health service:* There is no charge for most of the services of the health service, e.g. you do not have to pay to visit a doctor. At the same time supply is limited. At any moment there are only a certain number of doctors, nurses, hospitals, waiting rooms, surgeries, and operating theatres. Given that there is no price, there is excess demand. The only way of rationing this is the queuing system. People have to wait to be seen or have an operation because there is no price mechanism to ration off demand and increase supply. The problem of long waiting lists for operations is likely to increase: the population is aging which is likely to increase demand, especially since technology makes far more operations possible than in the past.

- *Indirect taxes:* Indirect taxes are taxes placed on the supplier and have the effect of raising costs.

There are two types
a ad valorem taxes which add a certain *percentage* onto the price
b specific (or per unit) taxes which add a fixed *amount* of money onto the costs.

Suppliers try to pass these increased costs onto the consumer. Their ability to do this depends on the relative elasticities of demand and supply.
- If demand is more inelastic than supply the consumers will pay the greater proportion (or incidence of taxation)
- If supply is more inelastic than demand the producer will pay the greater incidence of taxation.

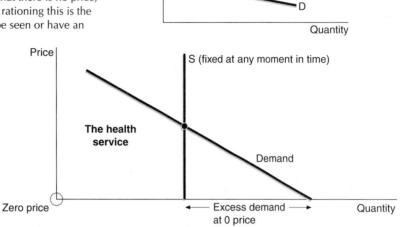

This good will not be produced – the highest price consumers are willing to pay (p_0) is less than the minimum price producers need to supply (p_1)

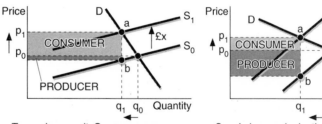

S (fixed at any moment in time)

The health service

Demand

Zero price

Excess demand at 0 price

Ad valorem tax — S_1, S_0, x%

Specific tax (per unit tax) — S_1, S_0, £x

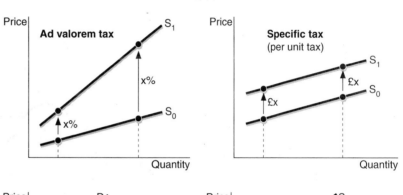

Tax = ab per unit. Consumer pays an additional p_0p_1. The rest is paid by the producer
Demand is more inelastic than supply so consumer pays greater incidence

Supply is more inelastic than demand so producers pay the greater incidence of tax

Tax yield when an indirect tax is first introduced, the yield automatically increases because there was none to begin with. When increasing the tax the yield will not necessarily increase:
- when indirect taxes are increased, the yield will increase if demand and supply are relatively inelastic.
- if a indirect tax is increased and demand and supply are relatively elastic, the yield will fall. Although the tax per unit is higher, the fall in the number bought reduces the overall revenue to the Government.
To maximize revenue the Government can widen the tax base, i.e. tax more goods and services; by taxing more goods the consumers will find it less easy to switch to a cheaper alternative and so demand is inelastic.

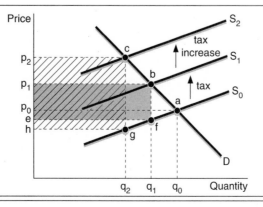

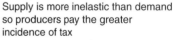

A tax is placed on producers, supply shifts S_0 to S_1. Tax revenue for the Government is p_1 bfe. Tax is increased, supply shifts S_1 to S_2. Tax revenue is now p_2 cgh. Revenue (or yield) has increased because demand is inelastic

Agricultural markets (primary products)

Producers in agricultural markets face two problems:
- long run downward trend in prices
- short run price instability

Long run downward trend
- supply is increasing due to better technology, e.g. fertilisers, machinery
- demand is not growing fast as demand is income inelastic

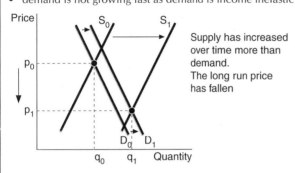

Supply has increased over time more than demand.
The long run price has fallen

Short run price instability
- inelastic demand because food is a necessity
- inelastic short run supply (e.g due to difficulties holding stocks; long production period)
- supply is vulnerable to sudden shifts, e.g. changes in the weather

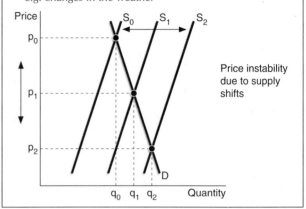

Price instability due to supply shifts

Price instability and incomes
Unstable prices also mean unstable incomes for farmers. If demand is inelastic it also means that farmers earn more in bad years than in good ones; with a fall in supply, prices increase and farmers earn more!

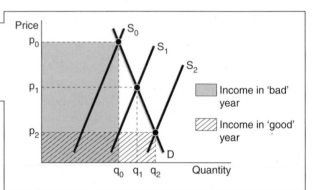

Income in 'bad' year

Income in 'good' year

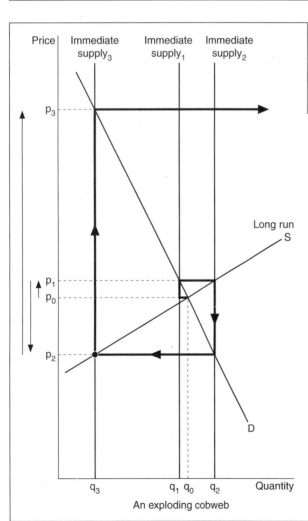

An exploding cobweb

The cobweb model
Highlights price instability in agricultural markets.
It is assumed that
- in the immediate run supply is totally inelastic; farmers cannot increase their output once a crop has been grown and taken to market until next season
- a farmer's decision about how much to produce next season depends on the price this season because it takes one season for the crop to grow, so they must plant it now (this is known as 'adaptive expectations')
- the long run supply is more elastic than the immediate run; this is because over time farmers can decide how many resources to devote to this crop and so can increase or decrease output.

Equilibrium is originally at po qo until a sudden supply shock, e.g. a natural disaster reduces the crop available to q1. Given the fall in supply the price rises to p1. Farmers then decide how much to plant next year; given the high price p1 they decide to supply q2. At the end of the next year q2 is produced; because this is much more crop than before, the price falls to p2. Farmers now look at the low price p2 and decide to cut back on production to q3. At the end of the next period they produce this and the price increases to p3. This is a signal to plant much more next period. This process continues:

- If the demand curve is more inelastic than the supply curve this causes an exploding cobweb, i.e. ever greater swings in the price level further and further from the equilibrium price.
- If the demand curve is less elastic than the supply curve it causes an imploding cobweb, where the price gradually moves back towards equilibrium.

Agricultural markets (primary products) continued

Buffer stock schemes

Prices are fixed at a given level (or within a specific range); if there is excess supply at this price the Government buys it up; if there is excess demand the Government sells its stocks.

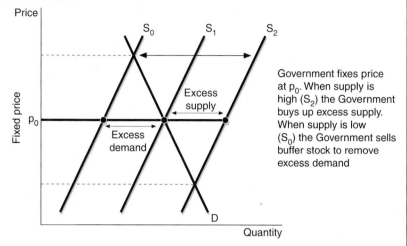

Government fixes price at p_0. When supply is high (S_2) the Government buys up excess supply. When supply is low (S_0) the Government sells buffer stock to remove excess demand

Problems of a buffer stock scheme

- storage costs
- some goods may be perishable
- administration costs
- if the Government sets the price too high (as it has in Europe) it is continually buying up crops - this has led to wine lakes and butter mountains. This is likely to be a problem as technology improves, so the equilibrium price should often be lower than the price originally set
- there may be inadequate supplies if there are many bad years
- to raise finance for this intervention, taxes have to be increased
- intervention in other areas of the economy might be more important

Guaranteed price scheme

The Government guarantees a price, e.g. p_1. Farmers therefore produce q_1. The market clearing price for this quantity is p_2 (i.e. this is the price at which this quantity is demanded) and so the Government pays a subsidy to the farmers equal to p_2 p_1.

Note: by allowing the market to clear, this system means the Government does not have to store the crops.

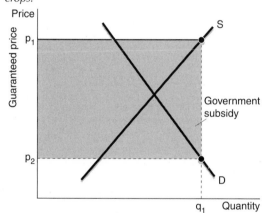

European Common Agricultural Policy

Aims to ensure supplies of food to the consumer within Europe and ensure an adequate return to the farmers. The European Union system taxes imported foodstuffs to increase their price to the level of European crops. It also runs a buffer stock scheme.

Set aside policy

This approach by the EU pays farmers for producing cereal crops on their land but insists they do not actually produce anything! This is to prevent excess supplies of grain throughout Europe, which the European Union would have to buy up.

Income support schemes

A scheme which keeps the price that farmers receive constant, still leads to unstable incomes. Alternatively the Government can stabilize income but this means prices will still fluctuate.

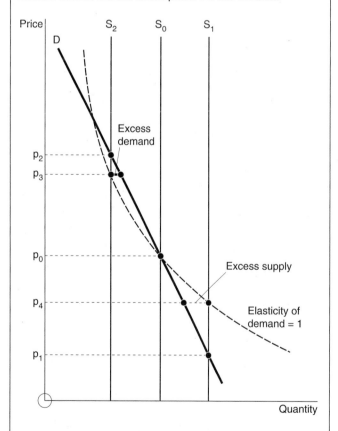

In a free market the price would fluctuate from p_0, p_1 and p_2 and incomes would fluctuate. Government sets prices from the unit elastic demand curve so that farmers' incomes are constant, ie p_3, p_0, p_4. When supply is S_1 Government sets price p_4. At this price there is excess supply; Government buys this up (buffer stock). When supply is S_2 Government sets price p_3. There is excess demand so Government sells buffer stock.

The market mechanism; failures and imperfections

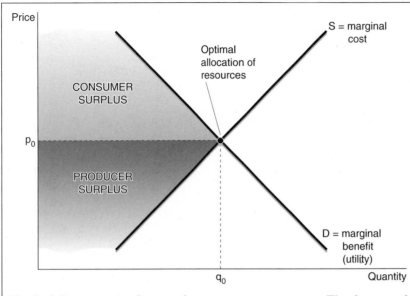

- **Consumer surplus** is the difference between the price the consumer is willing to pay and the price the consumer actually pays. It measures the utility which the consumer receives but does not pay for.
- **Producer surplus** is the difference between the price producers are willing to supply at and the price they actually receive.
- **Community surplus** is the welfare of society which is made up of consumer surplus and producer surplus.

  Community surplus = consumer surplus + producer surplus

Maximizing community surplus

Community surplus is maximized at po qo. This is the price and quantity combination which maximizes the area of consumer surplus plus producer surplus. Any other combination of price and quantity would give less overall community surplus.

The free market and community surplus

In a free market the price mechanism will bring about equilibrium at po qo and this is the combination of price and quantity which maximizes community surplus. This is why the free market is desirable and provides the optimal allocation of resources.

Market failures and imperfections

These are features of the free market which prevent it producing an optimal allocation of resources.

- **Market power**

  In a free market firms may come to dominate and have monopoly power. This can lead to higher prices and lower levels of output and cause a loss in welfare.

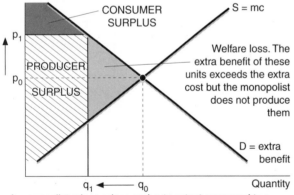

A monopolist raises prices and cuts output compared to a perfectly competitive industry.
Consumer surplus decreases; producer surplus increases; community surplus decreases (welfare loss)

- **Factor immobility**

  In a perfect market factors of production are able to move easily between markets. An increase in the demand for one product will lead to higher prices which will attract resources out of another industry. In reality there is often factor immobility. Resources cannot always move between industries. For example, if one industry declines and another is in a boom, individuals cannot easily leave one and work in another because they may lack the necessary skills; they may not even know the job exists (see occupational and geographical immobility).

- **Inequality**

  The free market may lead to significant differences in the income and wealth of different groups. Society may feel this is unfair and want to reallocate income to make it more equal. To achieve this the Government can tax higher income groups at a higher rate and pay subsidies to low income groups, e.g. in the form of benefits.

- **Merit goods**

  These are goods which are socially desirable, e.g. museums, libraries, education. (Note: this means our view of what is and what is not a merit good may change over time.) They can be provided by the market mechanism but to make them more available the Government provides them, subsidizes them or legislates to make consumption compulsory. **Demerit goods** are goods which society feels are undesirable, e.g. certain drugs. The Government legislates against demerit goods.

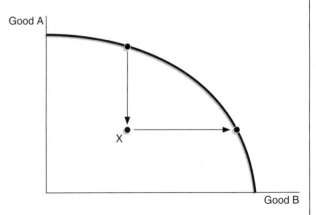

Resources come out of industry A but lack the skills or information to accept a job in industry B. Unemployment occurs at point X. This causes inefficiency

Market failures and imperfections continued

- **Externalities**
  An externality occurs when there is a divergence between social and private costs and benefits.

  With a **negative** externality, such as pollution, the social cost is greater than the private cost. Social cost = private cost + external cost.

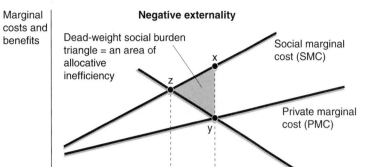

Negative externality

Marginal costs and benefits

Dead-weight social burden triangle = an area of allocative inefficiency

Social marginal cost (SMC)

Private marginal cost (PMC)

Social marginal benefit (SMB)

q_1 q_0 Quantity

Free market allocation (considering only private costs) is q_0. Optimal allocation is q_1. The free market overproduces. On units q_1 q_0 the social marginal cost > social marginal benefit, ie allocative inefficency

  With a **positive** externality, the social benefit is bigger than the private benefit.
  Social benefit = private benefit + external benefit

£

Positive externality

Potential welfare gain. On units q_1 q_0 the SMB > SMC; welfare would increase if they were produced

Social marginal cost (SMC)

Social marginal benefit (SMB)

Private marginal benefit (PMB)

q_0 q_1 Quantity

In the free market, equilibrium is q_0, because only private benefits are considered. The optimal allocation is at q_1 where social marginal cost = social marginal benefit. The free market underproduces by failing to take account of the external benefits

In a free market firms will base their decisions on private costs and benefits. They will not consider social costs and benefits. In the case of negative externalities they will overproduce; because firms do not take account of the negative external effect of their actions, they produce too much compared to the socially optimal level.

In the case of positive externalities the firm does not take account of the positive external effect of its action and so undervalues the output and produces too little compared to the socially optimal level.

Types of externality
- External costs of production
  A firm dumps waste into a river or pollutes the atmosphere.
- External benefits of production
  A firm trains its employees; these leave and go to work for someone else and, because they are already trained, it reduces the costs of the second firm.
- External costs of consumption
  By driving a car consumers increase the amount of pollution
- External benefits of consumption
  By listening to music, you not only give pleasure to yourself, but can also provide enjoyment for others.

Government Intervention
- Negative externalities: the Government can legislate to reduce output, e.g. to reduce noise levels, to limit pollution; the Government can tax firms to try to make their private costs equal the social costs (e.g. by taxing leaded petrol more than unleaded) - this is known as 'internalizing externalities'.
- Positive externalities: the Government can legislate, e.g. all children must go to school until the age of 16; or it can subsidize to reduce the costs and encourage more production.

Market failures and imperfections continued

- **Instability**
  The free market leads to instability in many markets. In agriculture, for example, shifts in supply due to natural occurrences such as the weather can lead to major movements in the price. To avoid this the Government might intervene using a buffer stock system. On a macroeconomic level, the economy often goes through cycles of booms, recessions, slumps, and recoveries. To avoid this instability the Government may intervene with fiscal or monetary policy.

- **Public goods**
  These are non excludable and non diminishable. Consumers cannot be prevented from consuming them once they are provided and additional consumers do not reduce the amount left for other people, e.g. national defence. Once a country is defended all of its inhabitants benefit automatically. Many public goods such as lighthouses could in theory be provided by the market mechanism but are not; these are called 'quasi public goods', rather than 'pure public goods'.
  Public goods suffer from the free rider problem. If asked whether they would pay for them, households would lie and say no because, once provided, they could benefit for free anyway. Because no-one is willing to pay for these goods (because they hope someone else will) they will not be provided in a free market. Therefore, the Government must provide them. (Note: for a 'private good', if one unit is consumed by one person it cannot be consumed by another).

- **Information problems**
  Consumers and producers do not always have perfect information. For example, restaurant and cinema owners do not know in advance what demand will be and so cannot change the price accordingly. This is why on some nights there may be empty seats; on other evenings there are queues. Producers in this situation have to estimate demand over a period and set an average price; on some occasions this will prove higher than the equilibrium price; on other occasions it will be too low.

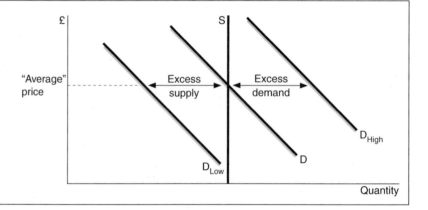

Government intervention in the free market
The Government can
- directly provide the goods and services, e.g. with public goods
- legislate, e.g. with merit goods such as education or demerit goods such as some drugs
- provide incentives or disincentives through taxation and subsidies, e.g. by taxing activities with negative externalities and subsidizing the provision of merit goods

Government failure
This can occur when the Government intervenes in the working of the free market. Public choice theory assumes governments attempt to maximize their self interest, e.g. get re-elected. This can lead to inappropriate intervention, e.g. short term policies not long term. There is also a danger of 'regulatory capture': regulatory agencies can be captured by the firms they are meant to oversee and then operate on behalf of these firms and not consumers.

Type of failure/imperfection	Consequence of failure/ imperfection in free market	Examples of intervention
public goods	not provided	Government provides, e.g. defence
merit goods	underprovided	Government subsidizes or legislates, e.g. education
demerit goods	overprovided	Government taxes or legislates, e.g. alcohol
instability	price fluctuations	buffer stocks
inequality	unequal income distribution, felt to be unfair	redistribution, e.g. taxes and subsidies
negative externalities	overproduction	taxes, legislation .
positive externalities	underproduction	subsidies, legislation
information problems	inappropriate pricing	attempts to improve information flow
market power	high prices, low output	legislation, e.g. competition policy
factor immobility	inefficient allocation of resources	training; improved information flows

Marginals, averages, and totals

Marginal
Marginal means extra, e.g. the marginal cost is the extra cost of producing another unit; the marginal revenue is the extra revenue from selling another unit.

Number of units	Marginal cost	Total cost
0	0	10 (fixed costs)
1	4	14
2	6	20
3	10	30
4	20	50
5	25	75
6	30	105
7	40	145

Marginals and totals
The marginal shows what has happened to the total, e.g. if the marginal cost of making another unit is £4, the total cost will increase by £4.

If the marginal is positive the total will increase. If the marginal is negative the total will fall.

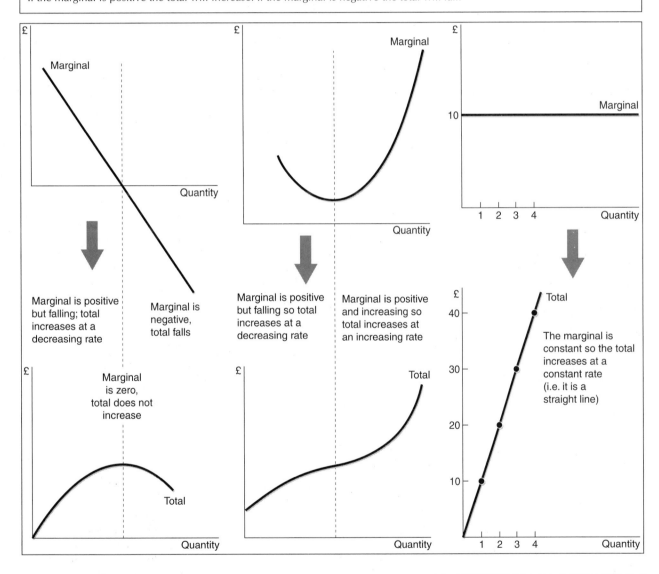

Averages and totals
To calculate the average, take the total and divide by the number of units,
e.g. the average cost is the total cost divided by the number of units. If the total cost of making 3 units is £9, on average they cost £3 each. If the total revenue from selling 4 units is £20, then on average the revenue from each one is £5.

Averages and marginals
If a marginal is above an average, the average will increase. Imagine that a team has scored 3 goals per game on average and in the next game scores 10. This will pull up their average. If marginal > average, then average increases.
If a marginal is less than an average, the average will fall. If a team has scored 3 goals per game on average and in the next game scores 1, this will pull down the average. If marginal < average, then average decreases.

Marginals, averages, and totals continued

Output and costs
The short run is the period of time when at least one factor of production is fixed.
The long run is when all factors are variable.

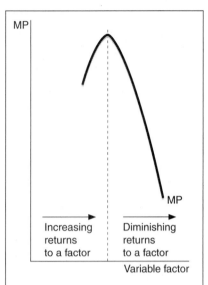

The marginal and average product
The marginal product is the extra output from hiring an additional unit of the variable factor. The average product is the average output per unit of the variable factor (also called the productivity of the factor).
Imagine the variable factor is labour. If the extra worker makes more units than the employees were making on average before he or she joined, the average output per worker will rise, e.g. if three workers make 9 units in total and the fourth adds another 11, the average will rise from 3 units each to 5 units each. If the extra worker makes less extra units the average will fall, e.g. three workers make 9 units in total (on average 3 each); if the fourth adds only 1 unit, the average is 10 divided by 4, i.e. 2.5 units each.

If MP > AP, then average product increases.
If MP< AP, then average product decreases.

This means the marginal product crosses the average product at the maximum point of the average product.

The law of diminishing returns (or the law of variable proportions)
As additional units of a variable factor (such as labour) are added to a fixed factor (such as capital), the extra output (or marginal product) of the variable factor will *eventually* diminish. (Note: the total output is still increasing, but at a diminishing rate.)

Assumptions of the law of diminishing returns
- at least one factor is fixed
- each unit of the variable factor is the same (e.g. each worker is equally trained)
- the level of technology is held constant

Number of employees	Total output (product)	Marginal product (MP)	Average product (AP)
0	0	–	–
1	10	10	10
2	26	16	13
3	39	13	13
4	48	9	12
5	55	7	11
6	60	5	10

In the table above we have assumed labour is the variable factor. At first there are increasing returns to labour, but with the third worker, marginal product falls and diminishing returns to a factor set in.

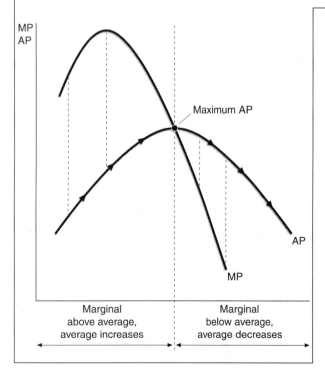

Output

Term	Explanation
Total product (TP)	total output produced by factors of production
Average product (AP)	the output per unit of the variable factor, e.g. output per worker
Marginal product (MP)	the extra output from employing another unit of a variable factor, e.g. the extra output from employing an additional worker

Productivity = output per factor, e.g. output per worker. Employees' productivity can increase with more training, more capital equipment, better management, improved technology.

Costs

Costs

- Costs include materials, labour, depreciation of equipment, the cost of capital and the opportunity cost of capital.

- **Marginal cost (MC)** is the extra cost of producing another unit.
  The marginal cost curve in the short run is inversely related to the marginal product - when the marginal product increases, the marginal cost falls and vice versa. Imagine the variable factor is labour. When each extra worker is more productive, less of their time is needed to make an extra unit. Assuming wages are constant, this means the extra cost of a unit will fall. When each extra worker is less productive, more of their time will be needed to make an extra unit and so the marginal cost of the unit will rise.

- **Fixed costs (FC)** are costs which do not change with output, e.g. the rent of a building is not related to output.

- **Variable costs (VC)** are costs which do vary with output, e.g. materials costs will increase if more units are produced.

- **Total costs (TC)** = fixed costs + variable costs
  $$TC = FC + VC$$

Productivity and costs are inversely related

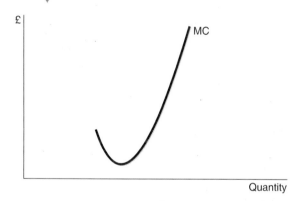

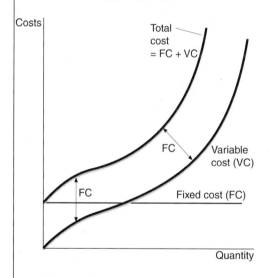

- **Average cost** = the cost per unit = $\frac{\text{total cost}}{\text{output}}$ = AC (also called ATC)

- **Average cost** (or ATC) = average fixed cost + average variable cost
  $$AC = AFC + AVC$$

Average fixed cost (AFC) – see page 26

Falls as more units are made - fixed costs are spread over more and more units.

Output	fixed costs	Average fixed costs
0	£20000	Infinite
100	£20000	£200
200	£20000	£100
300	£20000	£66.66
400	£20000	£50

Average variable cost (AVC) – see page 26

Generally 'U'shaped. On average the variable factor becomes more productive at first and then becomes less productive (see the average product curve). The average cost of the variable factor per unit of output falls when the factor is more productive and rises when the factor is less productive.

Average cost (AC) (also called average total cost (ATC)) – see page 26

Summation of the average fixed cost and the average variable cost. As more units are produced, the average fixed cost declines and so the average total cost is increasingly made up of the average variable cost (i.e. the ATC and the AVC converge).

Costs continued

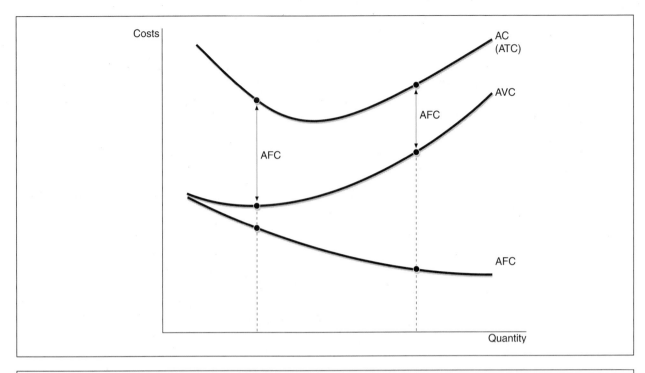

Marginal costs and average costs

If the extra cost of making a unit (the marginal cost) is greater than the cost of a unit on average, this will increase the average cost, e.g. if each unit costs £5 to make and the next one costs £20, the average cost will rise.

If the extra cost of making a unit (the MC) is less than the cost per unit, the average cost will fall, e.g. if the average cost of a unit is £5 and the firm produces an extra one for £1 this will bring down the average cost.

So if   **MC > AC, then AC rises**
If   **MC < AC, then AC falls**

This means that the marginal cost crosses the average cost at its minimum point.

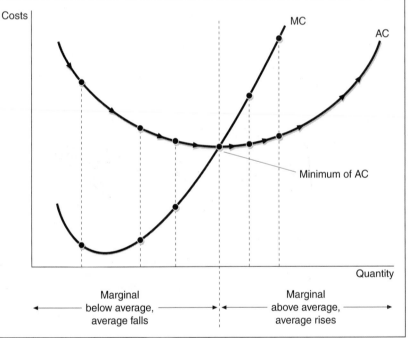

Costs

Total costs	fixed costs + variable costs	FC + VC
Average cost	$\dfrac{\text{total costs}}{\text{output}}$	$\dfrac{TC}{Q}$
Average variable cost	$\dfrac{\text{variable cost}}{\text{output}}$	$\dfrac{VC}{Q}$
Average fixed cost	$\dfrac{\text{fixed cost}}{\text{output}}$	$\dfrac{FC}{Q}$
Marginal cost	$\dfrac{\text{change in total cost}}{\text{change in output}}$	$\dfrac{\Delta \text{ in TC}}{\Delta \text{ in Q}}$

Long run cost curves

Long run cost curves
In the long run all factors of production are variable.

From short run cost curves to long run cost curves
A short run average cost (SRAC) shows the minimum cost per unit for different levels of output given a fixed factor, e.g. given 10 machines. There will be an infinite number of short run curves depending on the constraint, e.g. one SRAC for 11 machines, one for 12 machines, one for 13 machines and so on. As the firm changes its fixed factor over time, e.g. buys another machine, this is shown by a new short run average cost curve.
- If when the firm expands it moves onto a new lower short run average cost curve it is experiencing internal economies of scale
- If when the firm expands it moves onto a long run average cost at the same level it is experiencing constant returns to scale
- If when the firm expands it moves onto a higher short run average cost curve, it is experiencing internal diseconomies of scale.

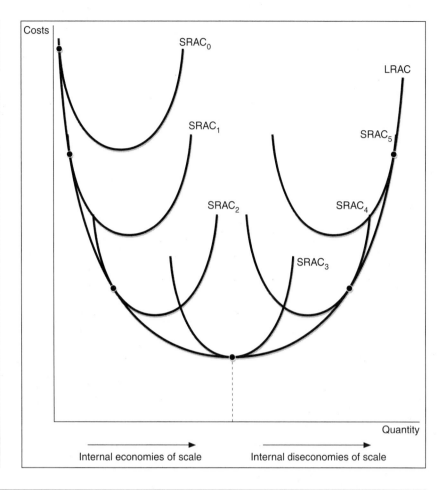

Internal economies of scale
- bulk buying. Larger firms tend to buy larger quantities of inputs and so are in a stronger position to negotiate discounts.
- managerial. The number of managers needed by a firm does not normally increase at the same rate as output, e.g. if the firm's output doubles, this does not mean it needs twice as many managers. This lowers the cost of management per unit. Also, as a firm grows, it will usually develop specialist management jobs, i.e. managers begin to specialize in different areas. This can lead to better decision making and more efficiency.
- technical. Some production processes are very expensive to run on a small scale. Imagine a car production line only producing two cars a week. By using the line to its capacity and making far more cars, the cost of the equipment can be spread over more units, lowering the cost per unit. Technical economies include:
  a specialisation - employees can be given specialist tasks to undertake; this should lead to higher productivity through repetition
  b indivisibilities - some pieces of equipment cannot be split up easily; they are indivisible, e.g. a production line. If the

line is only used to produce a few units, the cost per unit will be high; if it is used on a large scale to its full capacity the cost per unit will fall.
  c increased dimensions - if a container is doubled in size, the volume will more than double, making the storage costs cheaper per unit.
  d linked processes - most production consists of interlinked stages; the capacity of the machines at each stage may vary, e.g. machine A may be able to make 40 units a day; machine B may only be able to make 10. If only one machine A and one B is bought, A will be under utilised. If 4 B machines are bought the firm can produce 40 units and not have excess capacity.
- financial economies. Larger firms are often able to borrow money at a cheaper rate; this is because they have more assets and so it is less risky to lend to them.
- risk bearing economies. By diversifying into several regions or countries, the firm is likely to have more stable demand patterns. Sudden falls in demand for the product in one area are likely to be offset by increases in demand elsewhere. As a result, demand is more predictable and the firm does not need to hold as much stock just in case. This reduces stockholding costs.

Internal diseconomies of scale
Occur when the unit (or average) cost per unit rises with more output.
This may be because of:
- poor communications
- low morale; employees may feel alienated as the company grows and the gap between 'top' and 'bottom' grows
- lack of control

Long run cost curves continued

Minimum efficient scale (MES) This is the first level of output at which the cost per unit is minimized.

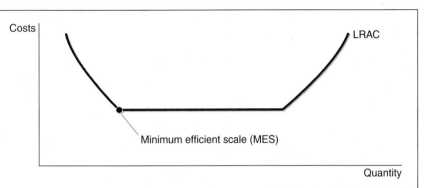

Returns to scale
These occur in the long run when all factors of production can be altered.
- Increasing returns to scale mean that a proportionate increase in all factors of production leads to a more than proportionate increase in output. For example, if the amount of land, labour and capital the firm uses is doubled, this will lead to an increase in output which is more than double. As a result, the cost per unit falls.
- Decreasing returns to scale occur when a proportionate increase in all factors of production leads to a less than proportionate increase in output. This leads to an increase in the average cost.

- Constant returns to scale occur when a proportionate increase in all factors of production leads to a proportionate increase in output, e.g. if all factors of production are doubled, output doubles. The cost per unit stays constant.

Increasing returns to scale v. economies of scale
Economies of scale refer to a fall in the <u>cost</u> per unit. Increasing returns to scale refer to changes in <u>output</u>. Increasing returns to scale contribute to economies of scale but one measures costs, the other output.

Cost minimization: least cost combination of factors
To minimize costs, firms hire resources where

$$\frac{MP\ labour}{price\ of\ labour} = \frac{MP\ capital}{price\ of\ capital} = \frac{MP\ land}{price\ of\ land}$$

i.e. the extra output per pound of each factor of production is equal. If the last unit of labour was more productive per pound than, say, capital, the firm will hire more labour and less capital.

External economies of scale
Occur when the cost per unit at every level of output is reduced because of factors outside of the firm, such as
- economies of agglomeration, e.g. if a firm is based in a particular area with other firms in the same industry, they can share resources (e.g. research or distribution) and specialist supplier firms may set up, supplying goods more cheaply.
- or if the suppliers grow larger, they may benefit from internal economies of scale. This will lead to cheaper inputs for a firm and reduce costs.

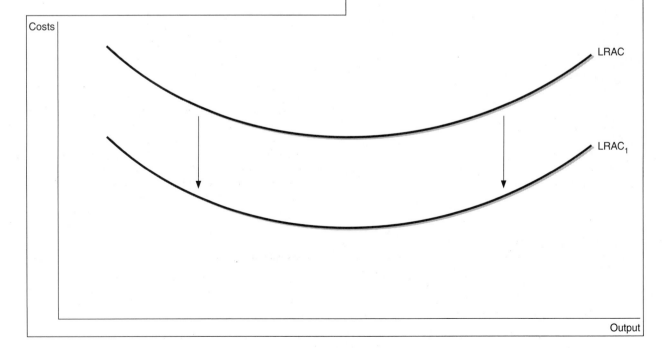

Price and output decisions

The marginal condition

This shows firms where to produce, i.e. what level of output to produce.

- If the extra revenue from selling a unit (the marginal revenue) is greater than the extra cost (the marginal cost) the firm will make extra profit by selling the unit. It should always make units where extra profit can be made (assuming it is aiming to profit maximize).
- When the extra revenue from selling a unit equals the extra cost from producing it (i.e. MR = MC) the firm must be making the maximum profit possible because no extra profit can be made.
- If the extra revenue is less than the extra cost the firm should cut back because a loss is being made on this extra unit.

To maximize their profits, firms should produce where marginal revenue = marginal cost

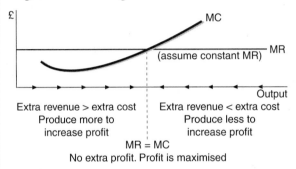

The average condition

This shows the firm how much profit (or loss) it is making at a given level of output.

To calculate a firm's profits look at the average revenue per unit (or price) and the average cost. The difference between these is the profit per unit. If we multiply this by the number of units we get the total profit (or loss).

- If the average revenue is greater than the average cost the firm is making an abnormal profit on each unit.
- If the average revenue is less than the average cost the firm is making a loss on each unit.
- If the average revenue is equal to average cost the firm is breaking even on each unit and just making normal profit.

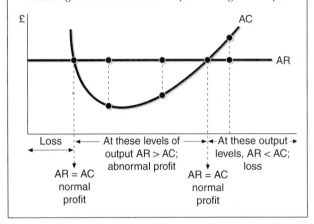

Profits

Normal profits

This is the amount of profit which is needed to keep resources in their present use in the long run. If the firms in an industry are making normal profit there is no incentive for them to leave or for other firms to join. Normal profit occurs when revenue equals cost. This is because the costs in economics include a reward to the entrepreneurs for being in that industry to cover the risk of being there.

Economic and accounting profit

There is a difference between an accountant's definition of profits, and an economist's view of profits. The economist includes a figure in the costs to cover the risk of the firm being in that industry and give a reward to the entrepreneur. If the firm were not making this amount, it would leave and join another industry in the long run. On paper, for example, a firm may make £200,000 accounting profit. An economist, however, may look at the firm's resources and the nature of the industry and claim that this amount must be made to stay in the industry. In this case, £200,000 is simply normal profit - the firm is just covering its costs (including opportunity cost).

Abnormal profit (or super normal profit)

This is profit in excess of normal profit. If firms in an industry are making abnormal profit, there is an incentive for other firms to join the industry if they can. Abnormal profit occurs when the revenue is greater than the costs.

Losses occur when the revenue is less than the cost.

Producing in the short run and long run

In the short run firms may stay in the industry even if they are making a loss.

This is because of fixed costs. In the short run, fixed costs must be paid, even if the firm is closed down, e.g. even if output is zero, the firm may be committed to paying rent. Therefore, if the firm stops production, it will make a loss equal to its fixed costs. If it produces, it starts to incur variable costs. Provided the revenue can pay for these variable costs, it is worth producing. If the revenue more than covers the variable costs, the firm is gaining a contribution to fixed costs, i.e. the loss by producing would be smaller than by closing down.

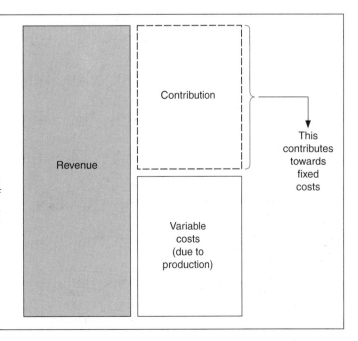

Price and output decisions continued

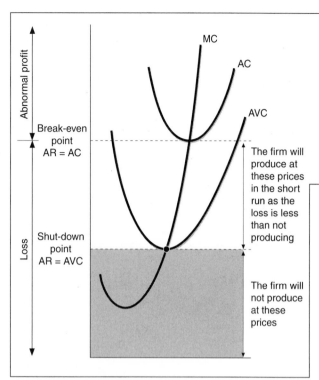

Short run production decision

In the short run a firm will produce provided revenue is greater than or equal to variable costs. In terms of each unit, this means it will produce provided
average revenue (which is price) is greater than or equal to average variable cost

Long run production decision

In the long run the firm will only produce if revenue is greater than or equal to cost (i.e. at least normal profits). Per unit this means that
average revenue must be greater than or equal to average cost

---

Efficiency

Pareto optimality includes:

- Productive efficiency - when it is not possible to make more of one good without making less of another, i.e. the economy is operating on its production possibility frontier.
- Allocative efficiency - no-one can be made better off without someone else being made worse off.

If all markets were perfectly competitive without any failures or imperfections, the free market would lead to a Pareto optimal allocation of resources, i.e. the free market would achieve productive and allocative efficiency.

Efficiency at firm level

- **Allocative efficiency**
  This occurs at the output where the social marginal benefit equals the social marginal cost (SMB = SMC).

If the social marginal benefit is greater than the social marginal cost, society would gain by producing an extra unit. The firm should keep producing until the two are equal, i.e. the extra benefit just equals the extra cost.

If the social marginal cost is greater than the social marginal benefit, society would gain by producing less of this good.

If the price reflects the social marginal benefit of a unit, then allocative efficiency occurs when the firm produces where
Price = marginal cost

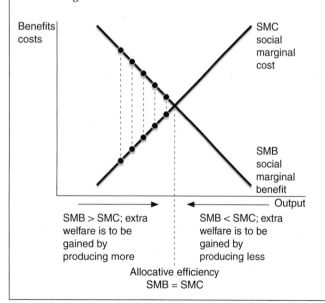

If P > MC then the benefit from an extra unit exceeds the extra cost
If P < MC then the extra benefit is less than the extra cost

- **Productive efficiency (technical efficiency)**
  Firms are productively efficient when they produce at the lowest cost per unit, i.e. at the minimum point of the average cost curve.

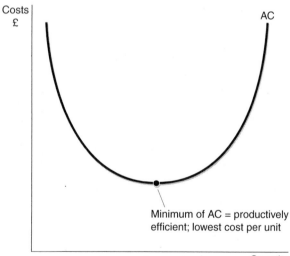

- **Dynamic efficiency** results from improvements in technical or productive efficiency which occur over time, e.g. new products, new methods of producing, new methods of management. Dynamic efficiency can increase with innovation, invention and research and development, investment in human capital.

Theory of second best

If a distortion or inefficiency exists in one market it is inefficient to treat other markets as if that distortion did not exist, e.g. if distortions exist, the Government may improve the overall welfare of society by introducing distortions in other markets.

Perfect competition

The assumptions of a perfectly competitive market are that:
- there are many buyers and sellers
- there is perfect information so buyers know what products are on offer and at what price

- the product is similar (homogeneous) so firms cannot differentiate their product
- there are no barriers to entry so firms can enter and leave the industry in the long run

- producers have similar technology and there are perfectly mobile resources (so one firm cannot maintain an advantage over another).

The firm as price taker

Each firm in perfect competition is a price taker. This means that changes in output by one firm do not shift the industry supply curve sufficiently to alter the price. If the whole industry makes more or less output the supply will shift and the price will change but not if <u>one</u> firm increases or decreases output. This means each firm can sell all it wants at the given market price. This also means that marginal revenue equals price.

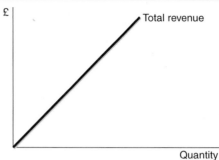

Each unit can be sold for the same price in a perfectly competitive market; MR is constant so TR increases by a constant amount, i.e. it is a straight line

The short run and long run in perfect competition

In the short run firms in perfectly competitive markets can make abnormal profits or losses. In the long run they can only make normal profits.
- if firms are making abnormal profits, other firms will enter the market in the long run. This will shift supply to the right and lead to a fall in price. This will continue until only normal profits are earned, e.g. price falls from p_0 to p_1.

- if firms are making losses, they will leave the industry, shifting the industry supply to the left. This will cause the price to increase. This will continue until the firms left in the industry are making normal profit e.g. the price increases from p2 to p1.

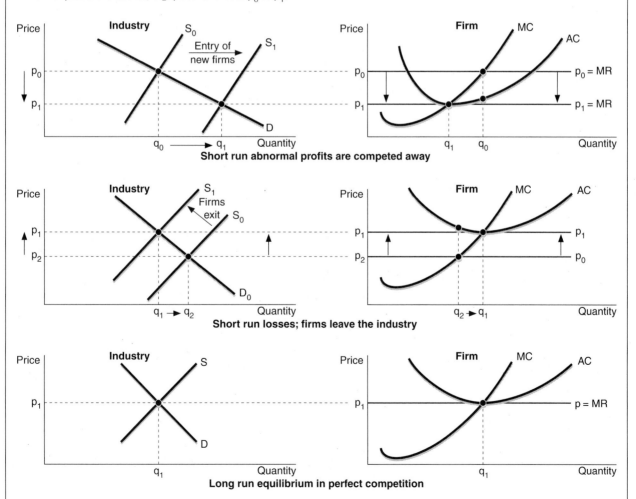

Short run abnormal profits are competed away

Short run losses; firms leave the industry

Long run equilibrium in perfect competition

Perfect competition continued

The supply curve

A profit maximizing firm will produce where marginal revenue = marginal cost. At this level of output there is no extra profit to be gained so the firm is profit maximizing.

In perfect competition the price is equal to the marginal revenue because each unit is sold for the same price.

So, $P = MR$

and to profit maximize, $MR = MC$

This means: $P = MC$

i.e. the firm will produce where the price equals the marginal cost. This means that given a particular price the MC curve shows how much is to be supplied - it is the supply curve.

Long run industry supply curves

- **Constant cost industries**
  Long run supply curve is horizontal. Demand increases, price rises, and existing firms make abnormal profit; this is an incentive for other firms to enter, shifting supply to the right until the price returns to its old level.
- **Decreasing cost industries**
  When firms enter they bring with them new technology; or the increase in the size of the industry allows suppliers to gain economies of scale, reducing costs. The new equilibrium price is below the old level. The long run supply is downward sloping.
- **Increasing cost industries**
  When firms enter input prices are bid up; the new equilibrium price is above the old equilibrium price; the long run supply is upward sloping.

Note: there is no supply curve in monopoly; there are no unique price and output combinations; firms can produce different quantities at the same price or the same quantity at different prices, depending on cost and demand conditions.

Short run supply

In the short run the price must cover average variable cost to produce so the supply is the marginal cost above the average variable cost.

Long run supply

In the long run the firm must cover the average cost to produce so the supply curve is the marginal cost above the average cost.

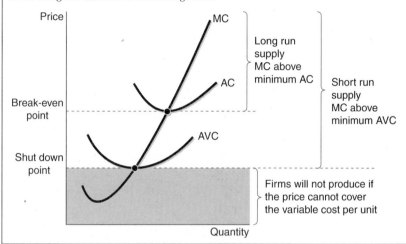

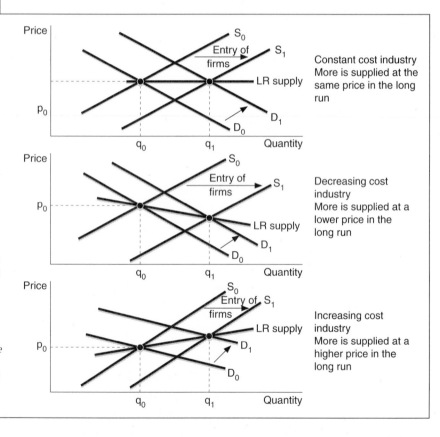

Constant cost industry
More is supplied at the same price in the long run

Decreasing cost industry
More is supplied at a lower price in the long run

Increasing cost industry
More is supplied at a higher price in the long run

Why are perfectly competitive markets desirable?

- in the long run firms only make normal profits
- firms are allocatively efficient because they produce where the extra benefit of a unit (represented by the price consumers are willing to pay for it) equals the extra cost, e.g. $P = MC$

- productively efficient, i.e. firms produce at the minimum of the average cost curve; this is the lowest possible cost per unit
- if a firm becomes more efficient than the others it can earn abnormal profit in the short run; there is an incentive for firms to innovate and become more efficient

But
- firms may not be able to afford research and development because they do not earn abnormal profits in the long run
- there is a lack of variety for consumers because the products are not differentiated

Monopoly

A monopoly exists where there is a single seller in a market.

A monopolist is a price taker. The monopolist faces a downward sloping demand and can set the price or the output but not both. If the monopolist sets the price it must accept the quantity that is demanded at this price; if it sets the output it must accept the price it can get for this quantity.

In a monopoly situation we assume that the firm is faced with a downward sloping demand curve and must lower the price to sell an additional unit. In the situation of a single price monopolist, only one price can be charged for all the goods, so if the price is lowered on the last unit it must also be lowered on the ones before.

Imagine the firm was selling one unit for £10. To sell another unit, the price must be lowered to, for example £9. The firm's revenue for two units is £18 (9 x 2) compared to £10 for one. Its marginal revenue is therefore £8 (£18 - £10). The firm has gained £9 on the second unit which was not sold before but lost £1 on the first unit which was previously sold for £10.

Similarly, if the price of two units is £9 each, the firm may have to lower the price to £8 to sell three units. The revenue is now 3 x £8 = £24 compared to 2 x £9 = £18, i.e. the marginal revenue is £6. The firm has gained £8 on the third unit but lowered the price of the two units before by £1 each, meaning it loses £2.

In each case the firm is gaining revenue from the sale of the extra unit but losing revenue on the ones before, where the price has been lowered.

Quantity demanded	Price (£)	Total revenue = price × quantity (£)	Marginal revenue (£)
1	10	10	–
2	9	18	8
3	8	24	6
4	7	28	4
5	6	30	2
6	5	30	0
7	4	28	–2
8	3	24	–4

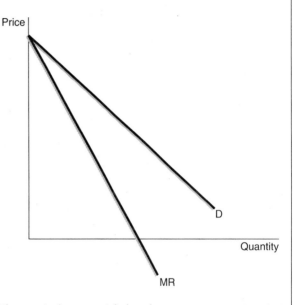

The marginal revenue is below the average revenue (or price) line and gets further away from it as more units are sold. This is because the price is continually being reduced on all the units before.

Marginal revenue and total revenue

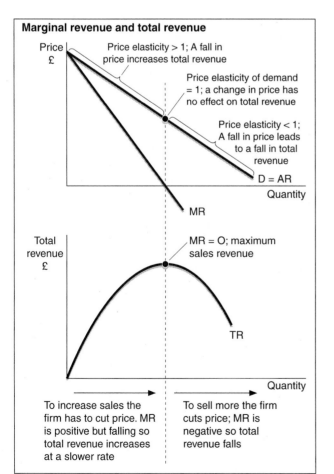

Price elasticity > 1; A fall in price increases total revenue

Price elasticity of demand = 1; a change in price has no effect on total revenue

Price elasticity < 1; A fall in price leads to a fall in total revenue

D = AR

MR

MR = O; maximum sales revenue

TR

To increase sales the firm has to cut price. MR is positive but falling so total revenue increases at a slower rate

To sell more the firm cuts price; MR is negative so total revenue falls

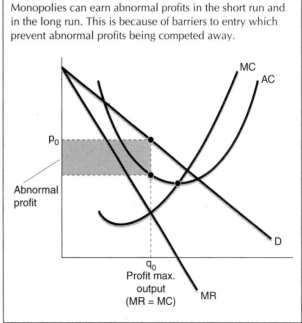

Monopolies can earn abnormal profits in the short run and in the long run. This is because of barriers to entry which prevent abnormal profits being competed away.

MC

AC

p_0

Abnormal profit

q_0
Profit max. output (MR = MC)

D

MR

Monopoly continued

Barriers to entry

These prevent firms entering an industry in the long run.

- patents and trademarks - these provide firms with legal protection for their ideas or designs which prevent other firms imitating them.
- control over supplies - if a firm has a monopoly control of the supplies in an industry, other firms will not be able to enter.
- a cost advantage - if a firm has a major cost advantage, e.g. because of economies of scale, other firms will not be able to compete.
- legislation, e.g. the Government may restrict the ability of firms to compete in a market. For example, for many years British Gas and British Telecom were Government owned and had monopoly positions.
- product differentiation - by making their product seem very different from the competition through their marketing and branding, a firm can establish a monopoly position.
- control over outlets so competitors cannot get their products to the market.
- fear of reaction of existing firms, i.e. other firms may not enter if they think this will trigger a price war.

Arguments in favour of monopolies

- The monopolist produces more than any single firm would in a perfectly competitive market. This may lead to economies of scale and, therefore, lower costs than in a perfectly competitive market. This in turn might lead to lower prices and higher output than perfect competition.

- The abnormal profits may be used to invest in research and development which may lead to cost saving innovations. Joseph Schumpeter argued that monopolists are a positive force in the economy - to gain a monopoly position firms often have to innovate; they then gain abnormal profits which encourage other firms to innovate in other areas to gain similar rewards and take away the first firm's market. This may be true in some markets but certainly not all monopoly situations.

- Competitive markets may over-produce, e.g. in the case of a negative externality - by restricting output the monopolist may actually improve resource allocation.

Arguments against monopolies

- The monopolist can earn abnormal profits even in the long run due to barriers to entry.

- The monopolist is allocatively inefficient, i.e. the price charged is greater than the marginal cost. This causes a welfare loss.

- The monopolist may be productively inefficient, i.e. it may not produce at the minimum of the average cost curve.

- Compared to a perfectly competitive industry with the same cost and demand conditions, the monopolist will charge a higher price for less output.

- X inefficiency - because a monopolist dominates a market, it may have less incentive to be efficient and keep costs down. Over time costs may rise because of inefficiency and complacency. This idea was put forward by Liebenstein.

Monopoly and efficiency

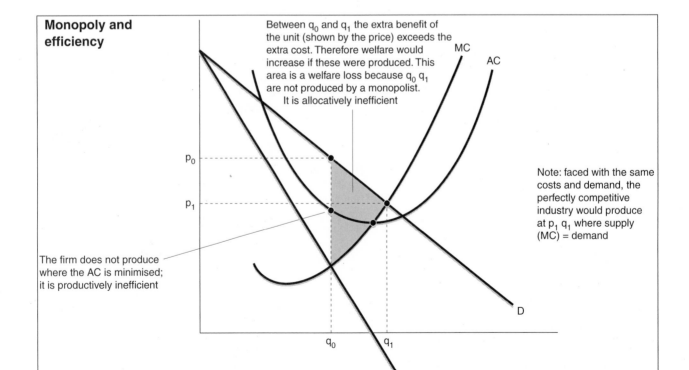

Between q_0 and q_1 the extra benefit of the unit (shown by the price) exceeds the extra cost. Therefore welfare would increase if these were produced. This area is a welfare loss because q_0 q_1 are not produced by a monopolist. It is allocatively inefficient

Note: faced with the same costs and demand, the perfectly competitive industry would produce at p_1 q_1 where supply (MC) = demand

The firm does not produce where the AC is minimised; it is productively inefficient

Monopoly continued

Natural monopoly

Large economies of scale; minimum efficient scale is at an output which is higher than the total demand in the industry.

One firm will keep expanding to gain economies of scale; other firms cannot compete due to cost disadvantages.

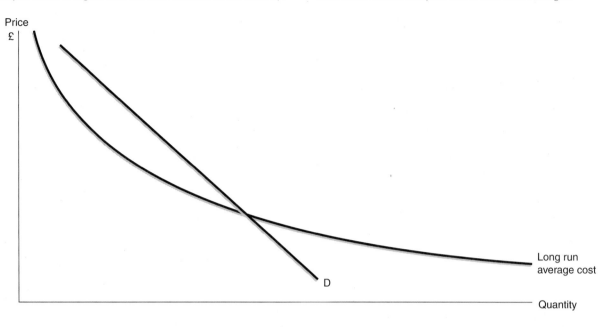

Control of natural monopolies

The Government may take over natural monopolies to control them. It may introduce marginal cost pricing to achieve allocative efficiency. If MC is below AC, the firm makes a loss and needs to be subsidized. Alternatively, a firm prices where price = average cost, so it does not make a loss.

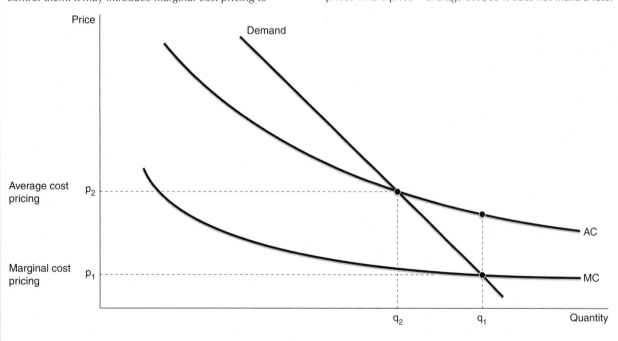

Contestable markets theory

Focuses on the threat of entry. What matters is not just whether competition exists at the moment but also whether it may exist in the future, i.e. how likely is it that other firms will enter - is the market contestable or not? If there is a high threat of other firms entering (even if they are not there yet) the existing firm will be forced to cut prices and produce as efficiently as possible, i.e. even if the market is a monopoly at present, the threat of others entering means the firm is behaving as if the market was competitive.

Need to consider entry and exit costs. Low entry and low exit costs make a market more contestable.

Monopolistic competition and price discrimination

Many sellers with differentiated products, e.g. shoe producers or restaurants.
In the short run firms can make abnormal profit. In the long run other firms will be attracted by the abnormal profits; demand for any one firm will fall until only normal profits are made.
In the long run the firm is
- allocatively inefficient because the price the consumer is willing to pay is greater than the extra cost of production (P > MC).
- productively inefficient because the firm is not producing at the lowest cost per unit, i.e. not at the minimum of the average cost.

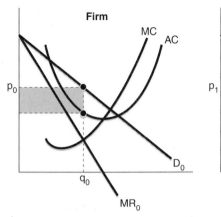

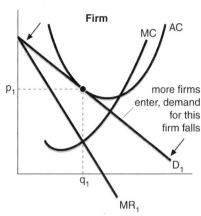

more firms enter, demand for this firm falls

Short run monopolistic competition
Abnormal profits (shaded area)

Long run monopolistic competition
Normal profits

Price discrimination involves charging different prices for the same good or service which have the same costs of production, e.g. charging a pensioner and student different amounts to use the same train.
To price discriminate a firm must

- be able to keep the markets separate, i.e. prevent individuals in one market buying at the lower price in the other market; it must also be able to prevent the people buying at the lower price from reselling at the higher price

- have some control over the price, i.e. it must be a price maker
- there must be different elasticities of demand in the different markets

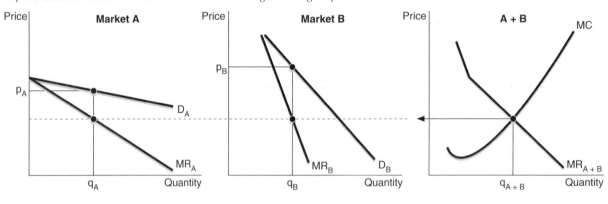

The marginal revenue in both markets is equal.
The higher price is charged in the price inelastic market

Methods of discrimination
- by time, i.e. different rates at different times of day (e.g. taxi firms/rail fares)
- by geography - different rates in different regions
- by branding, e.g. some firms sell their products under their own brand name and then also under a supermarket's brand name at a lower price

Advantages of price discrimination
Allows the firm to make more revenue from a given output. This may mean the firm can afford to provide some services which otherwise could not have been provided. This may benefit the consumer, e.g. a surgeon may charge some clients a high rate and so be able to provide lower rates for other clients.

Perfect price discrimination
The consumer is charged the maximum he/she is willing to pay for each unit. The price is different for *every* single unit. This removes all consumer surplus.

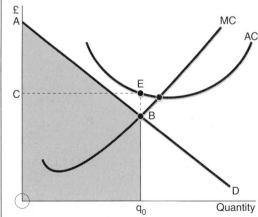

A different price is charged for each unit. Revenue is ABq_0O. Costs are CEq_0O. The firm can produce and make a profit. Whereas if it only charged one price to all customers, it could not make profit, i.e. could not provide the good or service

Oligopoly

An oligopoly occurs when a few firms dominate a market, e.g. the newspaper industry, supermarkets, airlines. (A duopoly occurs when two firms dominate.) Because there are only a few firms, the actions of one of them can have a significant effect on the behaviour of the others. There is no one price and output outcome in oligopoly. Firms are interdependent and a firm's behaviour will depend on what it thinks the others are going to do. Economists build different models with different assumptions; each will have its own price and output solution.

Competition and collusion
Oligopoly firms have two conflicting aims:
- to collude with other firms to maximize their combined profits
- to compete with other firms to take business away from them and make more profit independently

Kinked demand curve
We assume
- if the firm increases its price other firms do not follow so demand is price elastic
- if the firm decreases its price the other firms do follow so demand is price inelastic

This model explains price rigidity in oligopoly, i.e. why prices do not change very much and firms tends to compete via non price competition, e.g. advertising, sales promotions. This can be explained in two ways:
- If the price is increased, demand is price elastic and revenue falls; if price is cut, demand is price inelastic and revenue falls, i.e. any price change leads to a fall in revenue, and so the firm leaves price unchanged.
- The kinked demand causes a discontinuity in the marginal revenue curve; changes in marginal cost between MC_1 and MC_3 do not change the profit maximizing price and output, i.e. prices are likely to be relatively fixed despite cost changes.

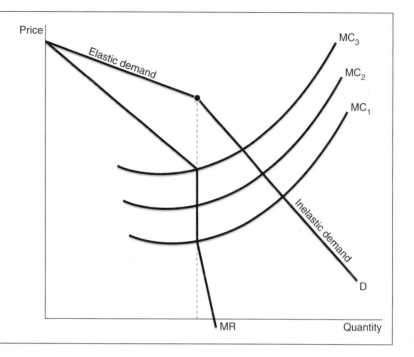

Collusive model (cartel)
Firms collude, i.e. work together and act like a profit maximizing monopolist. They fix a profit maximizing price and output and give each other quotas. This maximizes the industry's profits, but there is an incentive for individual producers to cut their price and exceed their quotas to increase their own profits at the expense of the industry, i.e. cartels tend to break down as there is an incentive to cheat unless there is an effective policing mechanism (an effective means of ensuring that firms are not producing too much or undercutting the agreed price).

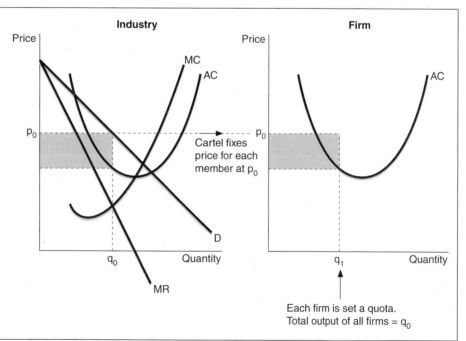

Each firm is set a quota.
Total output of all firms = q_0

What makes collusion more likely?
- if there are only a few firms, it is easier to check on each other and share information
- effective communication and monitoring systems mean that any cheating can be identified early on
- stable cost and demand conditions mean that quotas are easy to allocate and measure and the policy is easy to administer
- similar production costs so they make similar profits

Oligopoly continued

Limit pricing

This occurs when the existing firms in an oligopoly charge the highest possible price without allowing entry. Entry is prevented because firms realise that if they did join the industry it would force the price down and they would make a loss.

Price wars occur when firms in an oligopoly try to undercut each other. The aim is to force other firms out of the industry.

Price leadership

Sometimes in an oligopoly there is an obvious price leader, i.e. all firms follow the pricing decisions of one of the other firms. This may be because the price leader is the dominant firm in the industry and so the other firms do not want to challenge it by making different decisions. The decision to follow may be clearly agreed between the firms or it may occur without any formal agreement (this is known as 'tacit collusion').

Game theory

The decision that a firm makes in oligopoly depends on its assumptions about other firms. This means firms will try to calculate the best course of action depending on how others behave. Economists try to build models of this behaviour; this is known 'game theory', e.g. the prisoner's dilemma.

An example of game theory
Payoff matrix for pricing strategies of firm A and firm B

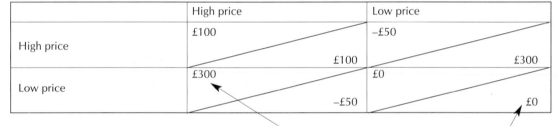

In the diagram above, the top left in each box shows the payoff for firm A, the bottom right shows the payoff for firm B.
If both firms co-operate and raise price they can both earn an extra £100; this is the most profitable outcome for both firms combined. However, if one firm agrees to raise price it is in the interests of the other firm to cut price. If firm A has a low price and firm B has a high price, for example, A earns £300 and B loses £50. If both firms fail to trust each other they will cut price and the end result will be that they both earn £0. The actual outcome depends on whether they can trust each other.

Non price competition

This is quite common in oligopoly. Rather than using price changes which can easily be followed, firms look for other means to compete, for example
- advertising
- branding, i.e. developing a well known brand name and brand loyalty
- sales promotions, i.e. offers (such as buy one get one free) and competitions
- distribution, i.e. controlling distribution to retail outlets

Role of advertising
- can inform
- can increase demand
But
- can mislead
- can create barriers to entry by making demand more inelastic, by shifting demand for other firms' products inwards, and by making the costs of entry higher

Market summary and competition policy

> **Concentration ratio:** the N firm concentration ratio measures the market share of the largest N firms, e.g. if the 4 firm concentration ratio is 80% this means the largest four firms have 80% of the market.

Types of market

	Number of firms	Freedom of entry in long run?	Nature of the product	Example
Perfect competition	many	yes	the same	wheat
Monopolistic competition	many	yes	differentiated	restaurants; shoes
Oligopoly	a few	no	differentiated	airlines; supermarkets; dominate newspapers
Monopoly	one	no	unique	British Rail used to be the only provider of rail travel in the UK; Durex used to have over 90% of the condom market; Microsoft dominate the market for PC operating systems (e.g. 'Windows 95')

	Abnormal profits?	Barriers to entry
Perfect competition	short run only	no
Monopolistic competition	short run only	no
Oligopoly	depends on the model	yes
Monopoly	short run and long run	yes

Competition policy

1948 Monopolies and Restrictive Practices Act
Monopolies are to be investigated on an individual basis. It is not assumed that they are always acting either for or against the public interest.

1956 Restrictive Trade Practices Act
Firms are obliged to register any restrictive practice agreements; these are assumed to be against the public interest unless those involved can justify them to the Restrictive Practices Court

1964 Resale Prices Act
Minimum resale prices are prohibited

1965 Monopolies and Mergers Act
Mergers can now be investigated

1973 Fair Trading Act
Created the Office of Director General of Fair Trading, who advises the Secretary of State. Monopolies can now be referred if they have 25% of the market (it used to be 33%). Nationalised industries can be investigated. Local and not just national monopolies can be investigated

1980 Competition Act
Aims to deal with anti-competitive practices by firms, for example
- predatory pricing - which involves selling products at a loss to drive out a competitor
- full line forcing - which involves making retailers buy the whole product range even if they only want one product
- exclusive supply, i.e. selling to only one outlet in an area

Competition policy in the UK is regulated by
- The Monopolies and Mergers Commission, which can investigate organisations which have over 25% of the market or a merger where the assets would exceed £70 million. The MMC makes recommendations about monopolies and mergers to the Director General of Fair Trading. The DGFT can order firms to cut prices, can prevent mergers, and can force companies to sell off assets.
- Restrictive Practices Court - this decides whether agreements between firms are legal, e.g. a price fixing agreement.
- European legislation is set out in Articles 85 and 86 of the Treaty of Rome.

UK competition policy is generally pragmatic, e.g. it appreciates the potential gains as well as costs of monopoly power, and investigates each case on its own merits.

Types of business

- Sole trader - an individual runs his or her own business; the owner is personally liable for any debts and has unlimited liability
- Partnerships - individuals work together and share joint responsibility for any decisions; unlimited liability
- Companies - a company has a separate legal existence from its owners; the owners have limited liability; companies are owned by shareholders

a private companies: have 'ltd' after their name; shares cannot be advertised
b public limited companies: have 'plc' after their names; shares can be advertised and traded on the Stock Exchange.
- Public corporations or nationalised industries are in the public sector

Integration - two or more firms coming together
- merger: two or more firms voluntarily join together
- take-over: one firm acquires another

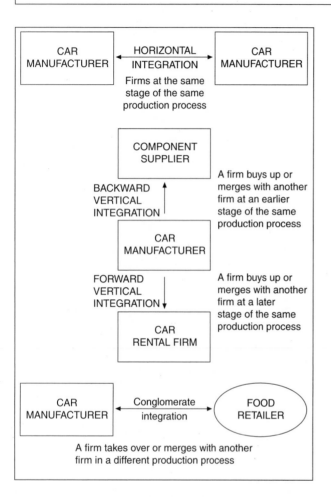

Managerial models
Managerial utility maximization (Williamson)
The owners of companies are shareholders. The people who control the company day to day are managers. In large companies, in particular, there is a divorce between ownership and control, i.e. the people who run the business are not the owners. This can lead to conflicting objectives. What the managers want to do is not necessarily what the owners want them to do. Given the fact that shareholders do not usually keep themselves well informed (or are not kept well informed), manager's often have considerable freedom in their decision taking. They may then pursue their own objectives and try to maximize their own utility rather than profit. Managerial objectives may include:
- increasing their salary - this may or may not be linked to profit (it is often linked to sales rather than profit)
- increasing the number of employees - this makes managers feel more powerful and important
- investing - this again makes managers feel more powerful
- getting additional benefits, e.g. a big office, first class travel, a bigger car

Sales revenue maximization (Baumol), (MR = 0)
Assumes managers want to maximize revenue rather than profit. *Why?*
- consumers value companies with increasing sales and are more likely to buy from them; consumers rarely know about the profits of companies
- financial institutions may be more willing to lend to a company with increasing sales
- salaries may be linked to sales

Growth maximization (Marris), (i.e. highest output where AR = AC)
Managers may seek to increase the size of their firm. *Why?*
- large firms are less vulnerable to takeover
- salary may be linked to size of the firm

Satisficing (Simon)
A firm involves or deals with many interest groups all with their own objectives, e.g. the different departments, the unions, suppliers, consumers, the local community.
The overall objectives of an organisation will be the result of discussion, negotiation and bargaining with all these groups. The end result is likely to be a compromise which reaches a satisfactory conclusion but which does not maximize anything. The firm aims to SATISFICE these different groups and still function.

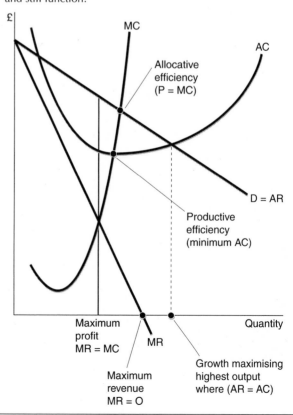

Labour

- **Derived demand:** the demand for labour is a derived demand. Firms only demand employees because of the demand for the actual goods and services.
- **Marginal product of labour:** the extra output produced by an additional worker. It will eventually fall as additional units of labour are added to a fixed factor because of the law of diminishing returns
- **Marginal cost of labour:** extra cost of hiring another employee

Demand for labour

The demand for labour is derived from the marginal revenue product of labour.

People are employed because of the value of their output. This depends on the extra output they produce (their marginal product) and the extra revenue this generates when it is sold (the marginal revenue).

The value of the output produced by an extra employee is called the marginal revenue product (MRP).

MRP = MP x MR

The MRP is downward sloping; MP slopes downwards because of the law of diminishing returns; MR also slopes downwards in an imperfect goods market or is constant in a perfectly competitive goods market.

The demand for labour will shift to the right:

- with more training, capital or better management, labour can become more productive
- if demand for the final product increases (i.e. MR increases)
- if the price of a substitute factor of production increases

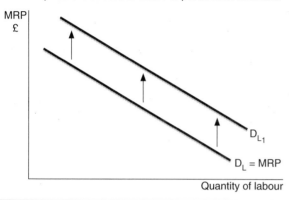

The elasticity of demand for labour depends on

- labour costs as a percentage of the total cost - the higher the percentage, the greater the impact of any wage increase and the more likely it is that the quantity demanded of labour will fall, i.e. the more elastic demand for labour will be.
- the time period - in the short run the firm may find it difficult to replace labour with other factors, e.g. capital equipment; over time it may prove easier and so demand will be more price elastic.
- the price elasticity of demand of the final good or service - a wage increase will increase costs and may increase price. If the effect of the price increase of the good is relatively small, the effect on the quantity demanded of labour is also likely to be relatively small, i.e. an inelastic demand for the product is likely to lead to an inelastic demand for the labour.

Individual's supply of labour

An individual can choose between leisure and work. If he/she decides to work more, then leisure time falls and vice versa. The decision whether to work or not depends on an income and substitution effect. For example, if the wage increases

- it is more expensive to have leisure time (because every hour you do not work you are giving up more money). The employee will therefore substitute towards work and away from leisure.
- at the same time more money is earned for every hour that is being worked, and so an employee might feel that he or she can work less hours and still have enough total income (the income effect).

Usually the substitution effect is greater than the income effect and people will want to work more hours when the wage increases. However, at some wages the income effect outweighs the substitution effect and people will decide to work less when the wage increases. This causes a backward sloping supply curve for labour.

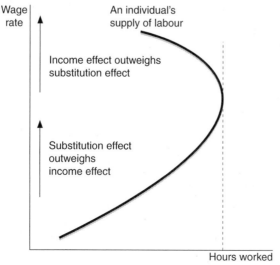

The supply of labour to an industry depends on

- the working population, e.g. population size, working age, and retirement age
- the non-monetary aspects of the job, e.g. job security, better working conditions
- the number of people who know about the job
- wages in other industries
- attitudes to work, e.g. attitudes towards women working in certain jobs

Hiring employees

Employees will be hired up to the point where the extra cost of hiring an employee is equal to the addition to sales revenue from hiring them (their MRP).

i.e. employees will be hired up to the point where MRP = MC labour

Labour continued

A perfectly competitive labour market

There are many firms and many employees; each firm is a wage taker, i.e. it can hire as many employees as it wishes at the given wage rate; a decision by one firm to employ more people will not shift the industry demand enough to increase the wage rate; although if all firms decided to hire more people, wages would increase.
In a perfectly competitive labour market, wages will be determined by market forces of demand and supply.

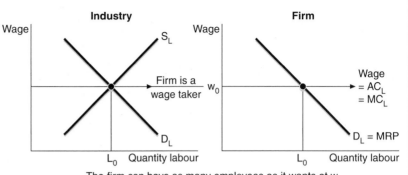

The firm can have as many employees as it wants at w_0.
The extra cost of an employee = w_0

Wage differences

In theory all wages will be equal because high wage rates in one industry will attract workers from another industry; this increases supply until the wage rates are equal.
However wage differences would still exist due to
- non-monetary factors, e.g. one job might be dangerous and so a higher wage is required to take account of this. The differences in the wages which take account of differences in factors such as working conditions and risk, is called the 'equalising wage differential'.
- labour immobility, e.g. geographical or occupational; this immobility prevents labour moving from one industry to another
- lack of perfect information, so employees do not know the jobs exist or what the wage rate is

Imperfections in the labour market

- imperfect knowledge - workers do not know what jobs are available
- immobility - workers cannot move from one job to another due to geographical or occupational immobility
- employers may not be profit maximizers - they may pay more than they need to; employees may not be rational economic maximizers, i.e. they may stay with a company out of loyalty even if they are 'underpaid'
- there may be monopoly buyers (monopsony) or sellers (unions)
- exploitation - this occurs when employees are paid less than their value. This happens when the employer is in a strong bargaining position, e.g. if the employer is a monopsonist (i.e. the major employer in the area)

Geographical immobility occurs

because people may have difficulty moving from one job to another in a different part of the country, e.g. because
- they have children in education and do not want to move them
- they have family and friends in the area
- it is too expensive to move (e.g. removal costs and house prices)

Occupational immobility occurs

when people cannot move from one type of job to another. This may be because
- they do not have the right skills
- they do not know the job exists

Problems with marginal productivity theory of wages

- difficult to apply in some labour markets - how is the productivity of a receptionist measured?
- in some markets, e.g. in the public sector, wages are set by the Government and not market forces
- it is circular - wages depend on the demand for labour, which depends on the demand for the good, which depends on wages

Wage determination in imperfect markets
Monopsony

This is a situation where the firm:
- is a major buyer of labour and has power over the market
- is a wage maker not a wage taker.
- faces upward sloping supply curves - they need to increase wages to attract more workers. They must increase the wage for the last worker and all the ones before; this means the marginal cost of labour is higher than the average wage rate (the average cost)

For example
3 workers are paid £200 a week each. Average cost of labour is £200.
To attract a fourth worker the wage must be increased to £300. The average cost is now £300. But the marginal cost is £600 - the new worker is paid £300 and each of the other three are paid £100 extra each. Looking at it another way: total cost was 3 x £200 = £600. It now is 4 x £300 = £1200, so the marginal cost of labour is £600.

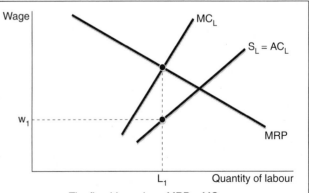

The firm hires where MRP = MC_L
Wage is w_1; number employed = L_1

The marginal cost of labour is, above and diverging from the average cost of labour; to hire more the firm must increase wages for the last worker and all the workers before.

Labour continued

Trade Unions

Trade unions are organisations which represent employees. Unions are established to protect employee interests and to bargain on their behalf. By joining a union, employees gain more strength in their bargaining.

Unions will typically bargain over issues such as pay, working conditions, and training.

Collective bargaining occurs when unions represent a group of employees. This gives the employees more bargaining strength with management.

Unions can affect the wage rate by
- improving productivity - by negotiating for better conditions and protecting the workforce, the unions may improve workers' output
- using industrial power (e.g. the threat of strikes) to force employers to pay more
- by restricting supply - in the past there have been closed shops in various industries and firms; this means that only union members are allowed to work there, which reduces the possible supply of labour and increases the wage rate.

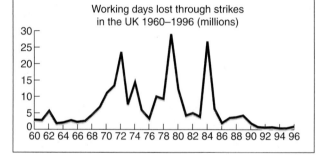

Working days lost through strikes in the UK 1960–1996 (millions)

Power over labour supply

Unions can use their power to push up the price of labour. This causes a surplus and reduces the number employed. Unions must decide whether to maximize the total wage bill, maximize the wages of those employed, or to maximize the number employed.

To try to increase pay and employment, unions must aim to increase productivity so that the demand for labour shifts outwards. This could be achieved through better working practices.

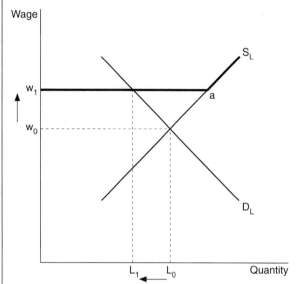

Unions may push wage up to w_1, i.e. labour will not be supplied below w_1. Labour supply becomes $w_1 a S_L$. Employment will fall to L_1.

Bilateral monopoly

This occurs when a monopoly buyer of labour faces a monopoly seller, e.g. a monopsonist v. a union. The outcome here depends on the bargaining strength of each side.

The power of trade unions depends on
- the number of members
- the legal environment - in the 1980s the Conservative Government considerably reduced the powers of trade unions; it made them more liable for the consequence of their actions and prevented industrial action without a secret ballot
- the demand for the product; if demand is inelastic, for example, the firm will be more likely to pay higher wages because it will be easier to pass on the higher costs to the consumer in the form of higher prices
- if labour costs are a small percentage of total costs - the effect of a wage increase will be smaller if labour is only a relatively small percentage of total costs
- if the firm is profitable - this means it may be more likely to pay more to employees compared to a situation where it was making a loss

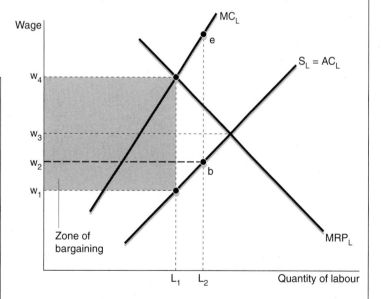

Monopsonist would hire L_1 workers at w_1. If union imposes minimum wage of, e.g. w_2, supply becomes $w_2 b S_L$. Firm can hire as many workers as it wants up to L_2 at a wage of w_2; after this point it would have to increase wages for extra workers and all the ones before. The MC curve is $W_2 b e MC_L$. The Firm will hire up to the point where $MRP = MC_L$, i.e. L_2 workers at w_2, i.e. the union has increased wages and employment. The union can keep doing this up to w_3. After w_3 (up to w_4) it can increase wages but employment begins to fall back towards L_1

Labour continued

Differences in individuals' earnings depend on
- ability and skills - the greater an individual's skill, the more he or she is likely to earn, e.g. if they are more trained or have achieved higher qualifications
- non-monetary characteristics of a job, e.g. people may have to be paid more to do a dangerous job
- age - earnings tend to increase with age up to a point and then decline
- gender and race - women and non whites tend to earn less; this could be because of a lack of training or discrimination
- location - wages vary across the country and between countries
- demand for the individual

Minimum wage

The impact of a minimum wage is greater when demand for and supply of labour are elastic

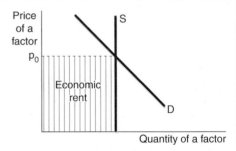

Inelastic supply of and demand for labour

Elastic supply of and demand for labour

- aims to help low paid
- may give more incentive to work
- may increase unemployment
- effect on employment depends on market structure, e.g. whether it is a monopsony
- might also deter foreign investment

Effect depends on
- how far above equilibrium the minimum wage is set (if at all)
- elasticity of supply and demand for labour

The increase in wages might
- increase demand for goods and services and for labour
- increase labour morale and productivity

Poverty occurs due to
- low earnings when employed
- poverty and unemployment traps
- unemployment
- lack of training and skills
- lack of benefits

Absolute poverty: having insufficient income to obtain the minimum means necessary for survival, i.e. basic food, housing, and clothing (Rowntree).

Relative poverty, i.e. relative to others, e.g. an inability to take part in the typical activities of society - this may include having a TV, a telephone, and a fridge (Townsend).

Transfer earnings
This is the amount that a factor of production must earn to keep it in its present usage in the long run.

Economic rent is payment over and above transfer earnings.

Quasi rent
Imagine a machine with only one use is purchased. Once bought all its earnings are economic rent, assuming it has no alternative use. Over time it will depreciate and will not be replaced unless it earns a satisfactory return; some of its earnings are now transfer earnings - if it does not make enough, a new machine will not be bought.

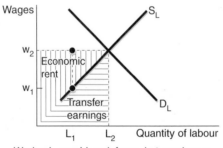

Worker L_1 would work for w_1 but receives w_2. w_1w_2 is 'economic rent'

Supply of the factor is completely inelastic; it has no alternative use; all of its earnings are 'economic rent'

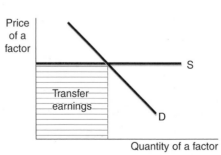

With a perfectly elastic supply all earnings are transfer earnings. There is no economic rent

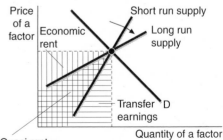

Quasi rent = economic rent short term; transfer earnings long term

National income accounting

Three methods of calculating national income:
- expenditure method
- income method
- output method

If £100 worth of goods has been produced (output) this has generated £100 of income for the various factors of production (income) and will lead to £100 of spending (expenditure). *Note*: if no-one else buys the goods, the firm will end up with stocks, and we count this as if it bought them itself.

OUTPUT = INCOME = EXPENDITURE

The expenditure method adds up spending in the economy.

C   consumers' expenditure
+ I   investment spending by firms; this includes planned investment in capital and unplanned increases in stock (listed as gross fixed capital formation and the value of physical increases in stock)
+ G   Government spending (usually listed as general Government consumption)
+ X   export spending
– M   import spending

Import spending must be deducted because it is spending on goods and services from outside the UK, i.e. this spending leaves the economy.

Adding up C+I+G+X-M gives Gross Domestic Product (GDP) at market prices

The income method

wages & salaries
+ self-employed income
+ trading profits
+ rent (includes 'imputed rent', e.g. the rental value of owner occupied housing is estimated and included)
+ interest
= total domestic income
less stock appreciation (if stocks increase in value over the year this exaggerates their value)
= GDP

Note: transfer payments should be excluded; these are payments for which no corresponding good or service is produced, e.g. social security payments.

Market prices to factor cost

If the spending of different groups in the economy is added up, this will show the spending at current or market prices. This does not reflect the income earned by the factors of production because:
- the market price is too high because of indirect tax
- the market price is too low because of subsidies

Market price - indirect taxes + subsidies = factor cost

The output method

i) Adds up the added value of every firm's output (i.e. the value of the output minus the value of the input); this avoids double counting, e.g. counting the value of the steel and the value of the car which also includes the value of the steel. Or **ii)** add up the output of <u>final</u> goods and services.

Gross Domestic Product (GDP) shows the value of final goods and services produced by factors of production within a country.

Gross National Product (GNP) shows the value of final goods and services produced by factors of production owned by a country's citizens, regardless of where in the world this is earned.

GNP = GDP plus net property income from abroad

Gross National Product to Net National Product (NNP)

Out of the income earned in the economy some will be spent replacing equipment that has depreciated. To measure the additional (or new or net) income earned, we deduct the amount spent simply on replacement of items.

Gross National Product
– Depreciation *(also called 'capital consumption')*
= Net National Product (NNP) *(also called 'net income')*

Summary

GDP market prices
+ net property income from abroad
= GNP market prices
– indirect taxes + subsidies
= GNP factor cost
– depreciation
= NNP

GDP 1996	£bn at 1990 prices seasonally adjusted
Consumers' expenditure	374.87
General Government consumption	120.3
Gross fixed investment	102.1
Changes in stocks	1.1
Exports of goods and services	177.7
Imports of goods and services	181.8
Adjustment to factor cost	76.8
Statistical adjustment	2.1
GDP at factor cost	520.2

Source Economic Trends

National Income figures £mn

	1985	1986	1987	1988	1989	1990	1991	1992	1993	1994	1995
GDP	307902	328272	360675	401428	441759	478886	496253	518132	547750	578607	603495
GNP	310198	332901	364602	405994	445261	480155	496403	521256	549947	587298	613067
NNP	268315	287816	316438	353358	388545	418894	433047	458771	484869	519287	540643

National income accounting continued

Problems comparing national income figures between countries

- the income figures of each country have to be converted into a common currency. It can be difficult deciding what exchange rate to use, because the value of the exchange rate is often changing all the time
- accounting techniques vary between countries, which can alter the way in which income is calculated
- it is important to take the price level into account, as well as the nominal income figure - a country may have less average income but also lower prices
- you should consider factors such as climate - one country may have to produce heat; another may get it for free
- the composition of output may vary considerably - one country may be spending in defence, another may be producing consumer goods
- the distribution of income is likely to vary
- some economies have much more barter and a greater black economy than others

GDP deflator

Real national income is calculated by adjusting national income figures for inflation. The Retail Price Index is not used as it only considers consumer prices; a more complex measure of inflation is used, called the GDP deflator.

Standard of living

Often measured by real GDP per capita.

real GDP per capita = $\dfrac{\text{real GDP (which is the GDP adjusted for inflation)}}{\text{population}}$

But

- this ignores the value of goods and services which are not traded, e.g. goods which are swapped in a barter economy; housework; the black economy (work which is not declared to the Government); DIY.
- it ignores the distribution of income - although the average real GDP per person may be quite high, there could be a few extremely rich people and many poor.
- it does not take account of what is produced - one economy might be producing capital goods, which involves less consumption now but should lead to more future growth; another might be producing consumption goods which involves high levels of consumption today but less in the future.
- there are problems comparing over time, e.g. the price of videos and personal computers has gone down over the years. This might reduce the value of national income, even though the quality of the goods and the number of features has improved.
- economic 'bads' can increase the figure even though the 'quality of life' has fallen, e.g. a traffic jam causes more consumption of petrol and increases the output and income of the country.
- valuation problems, e.g. some output such as defence or the health service does not have a market price; the value of these services is assumed to be the cost of providing them, which may over or under value them.
- the quality of life - if we take longer holidays or work less hours, output and income may fall but we may enjoy life more; similarly, tougher restrictions on pollution might reduce output but increase the quality of our lives.

Other indicators of standard of living

Given the problems using national income figures to compare standards of living between countries or over time, some commentators use other indicators, such as number of doctors per 1000 population, adult literacy, life expectancy.

Net Economic Welfare (Tobin and Nordhaus); measure of economic welfare;

adjusts GNP by deducting economic 'bads' (e.g. pollution) and adding the value of non marketed activities (such as barter) and the value of leisure.

Lorenz curve

This illustrates the distribution of incomes in an economy, e.g. in the diagram 30% of the families in the country have only 15% of the income. The Gini coefficient measures the income equality by measuring the area between the line of absolute equality and the line of actual distribution of income (see shaded area). The bigger this area, the more unequal the distribution.

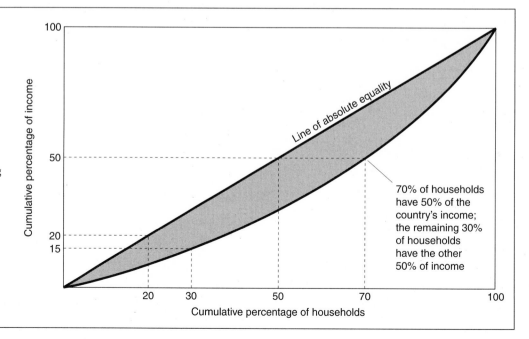

70% of households have 50% of the country's income; the remaining 30% of households have the other 50% of income

Aggregate demand

Aggregate demand is the total planned expenditure on final goods and services in an economy.
It is made up of:
C consumption spending by households
+I investment spending by firms
+G Government spending by the Government
+X exports spending from overseas
–M imports spending on foreign goods and services
Note: Import spending has to be deducted, because some of the spending in C + I + G is on foreign goods and services and so does not stay within the economy.

Aggregate demand will increase with
- an increase in consumption (e.g. due to lower income tax)
- an increase in investment (e.g. due to lower interest rates)
- an increase in Government spending (e.g. a budget deficit)
- an increase in exports (e.g. due to a lower exchange rate)
- a fall in imports (e.g. due to quotas)

Injections (J) represent spending on final goods and services in addition to consumers' spending. Injections increase aggregate demand.
Planned injections represent spending in addition to that of the households in the economy, e.g. spending by other groups such as the Government, firms, and overseas buyers, i.e. injections = investment + Government spending + exports
$$J = I + G + X$$

Withdrawals (W) represent a leakage from the economy. They represent income which is earned by households but which is not spent on final goods and services. Withdrawals reduce aggregate demand.
Planned withdrawals represent income which the households have earned which they do not want to spend within the economy. This could be because they want to save it (S), they have to pay it in tax (T) or they want to spend it overseas (M), i.e. $$W = S + T + M$$

Imagine the income in the economy is £100. This means £100 of output is produced and in a simple circular model this is all bought by households who earn £100 and spend £100.

Income (Y) £100
Factor services

Firms

Households

Goods and services

A simple circular flow

Consumer's spending (C) £100

In reality, households may not want to spend all of the £100 in the economy; they may withdraw £40 and only want to spend £60. In this case the level of demand in the economy is too low; £100 is produced but only £60 is demanded. Equilibrium will be restored provided the other groups (firms, Government and overseas buyers) want to buy up the £40 of output that the households do not want.
i.e. provided the planned injections = the planned withdrawals, there will be equilibrium.

If the other groups only want to buy £30 of goods, there will still be £10 left over. Aggregate demand is too low. Because the planned injections did not compensate for the planned withdrawals, demand is too low.

If planned injections is less than planned withdrawals, then aggregate demand is too low.
If the other groups had wanted to buy £50, demand would have been too high because there was only £40 of goods left over.
If planned injections are greater than planned withdrawals, then aggregate demand is too high.

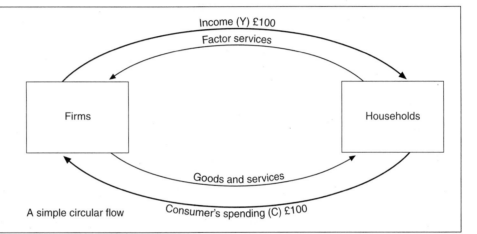

Withdrawals £40

Income (Y) £100

Firms

Households

Consumer's spending (C) £60

J injections £40

Equilibrium in the circular flow

Aggregate demand continued

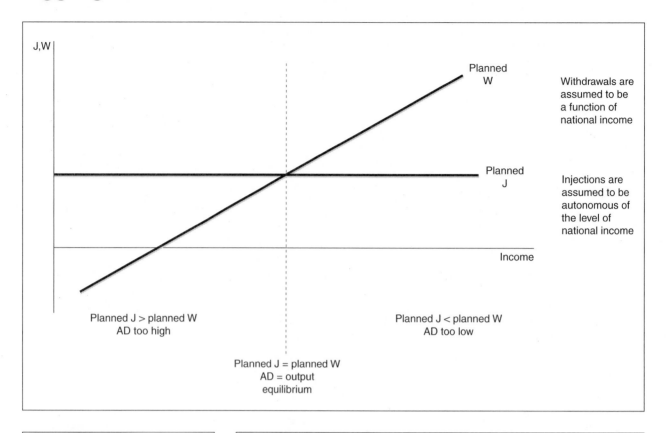

Types of economy
- Two sector: households and firms
- Three sector: households, firms, and Government
- Four sector: households, firms, Government, and trade
- Open economy: has trade
- Closed economy: no trade

The paradox of thrift
If households try to save more of their income, they may end up saving exactly the same amount of money as before! This is because if they save more of their money, this reduces the level of demand in the economy, which leads to a downward multiplier and a fall in the level of income. Although they may save a greater *proportion* of their income, because income has fallen their total savings in a two sector economy will be the same total amount as before (because for equilibrium, planned savings must still equal planned investment, which is unchanged).

Remember

$$AD = C + I + G + X - M$$

Consumption

The level of consumption in the economy is the planned level of spending on final goods and services by households. It is a major element of aggregate demand.

Keynesian consumption function

According to Keynes, the level of national income is a major determinant of consumer spending.

$C = a + bY$

where C = the level of consumption

    a = autonomous spending. This represents spending which the household would do even if income was zero.

    b = the marginal propensity to consume. This is the extra spending out of each extra pound and is given by the equation: $\dfrac{change\ in\ consumption}{change\ in\ income} = \dfrac{\Delta C}{\Delta Y}$

    Y = current income

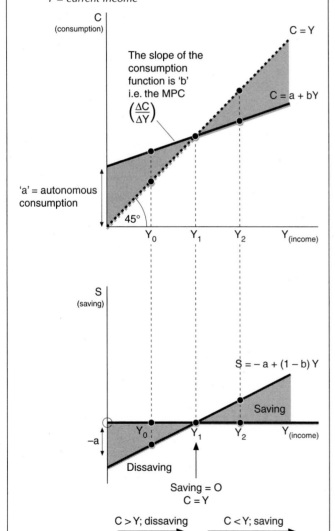

At income level Y_0, the level of consumption is greater than the level of income; consumers are spending more than they earn; this means they are dissaving.

At income level Y_1, the level of consumption = the level of income; consumers are spending all that they are earning; there are no savings.

At income level Y_2, the level of consumption is less than the level of income; consumers are saving.

The size of the marginal propensity to consume depends on:

- a consumer's level of income - usually we assume the mpc is constant, i.e. the consumer consumes the same amount out of each pound. In reality, as consumers earn more they are likely to save more out of each pound and spend less.

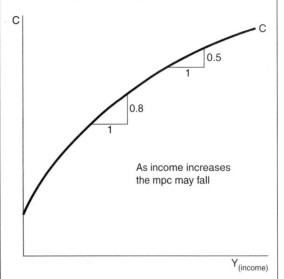

As income increases the mpc may fall

- interest rates - higher interest rates may increase the amount saved out of each extra pound and reduce the mpc.
- expectations of higher prices in the future might increase the mpc *now*.
- taxation - with higher tax rates less will be spent out of each pound.

Savings

Savings are related to consumption. If we are spending more of our income, we are saving less.

Levels of saving will depend on

- interest rates - if interest rates increase, there is a greater incentive to save.
- income levels - higher income groups are more likely to save out of each extra pound (they have a higher marginal propensity to save).
- inflation - with inflation, the purchasing powers of people's savings may be reduced (to maintain the same real level of savings they may have to save more).
- expectations - if people are worried about the future state of the economy and whether they will have a job, they may save more.

Discretionary and contractual savings

- With contractual savings, an individual agrees to save a certain amount each month, e.g. as part of a pension plan.
- With discretionary saving an individual may or may not save; they are not contractually obliged to.

Consumption continued

The average propensity to consume

The average propensity to consume shows the amount consumed on average out of each pound earned.

$$APC = \frac{C}{Y}$$

On a diagram, the APC is shown by the gradient of rays from the origin to each point on the consumption function.
The APC falls with higher levels of income. This is because when income is low the level of consumption is relatively high because of the autonomous element of consumption. As income levels increase, the autonomous level of consumption becomes less significant.

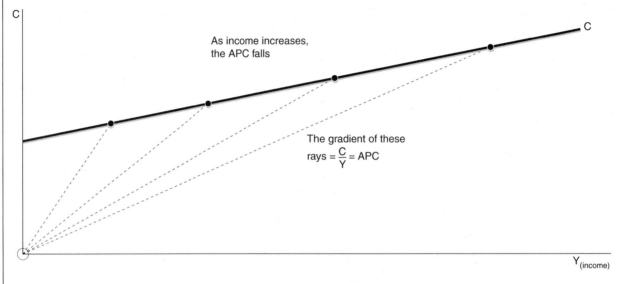

As income increases, the APC falls

The gradient of these rays $= \frac{C}{Y} = APC$

Income (Y)	Consumption (C) assume C = 10 + 0.8Y	Average propensity to consume (APC)
0	10	Infinite
10	18	1.8
20	26	1.3
30	34	1.13
50	50	1
100	90	0.9
500	410	0.82
1000	810	0.81

If there is no autonomous element of consumption, the APC = MPC.

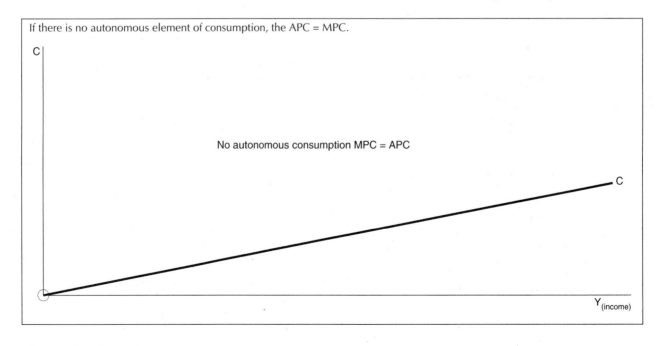

No autonomous consumption MPC = APC

Consumption continued

Other factors influencing consumption

- Relative income. A consumer's spending will be influenced by what others are earning and spending, and what they themselves have been spending in the past. Imagine that a household earns £20000, and spends £18000 p.a. The household then gets a pay rise and earns £30000 and spends £25000. If after several years that household's income falls back to £20000, its consumption will NOT fall back to £18000 in the short run. This is because the household has become accustomed to the higher levels of spending and many of their friends are probably still spending at that level.
- Expectations. Consumers' spending depends on what they think they are going to earn in the future. If they think their income is likely to rise, they are likely to increase their consumption now, even if their income has not gone up yet. If consumers expect prices to rise they will buy goods now and not wait.
- Interest rates and credit. If interest rates are low, there is less incentive to save and so consumers are more likely to spend. If credit is readily available, borrowing and spending may increase.
- Wealth. If consumers' wealth increases, spending may be high even if their income is low. In the 1980s, for example, the increase in house prices made many households wealthier and more confident about spending.
- The distribution of income. If income is redistributed and taken from high income groups and given to low income groups, consumption is likely to rise. This is because the low income groups tend to spend more out of each pound.

Other theories of consumption
Permanent income hypothesis (Friedman)
Households estimate their expected future earnings and divide these up over the remaining time periods to calculate their permanent income. Consumers then consume a proportion of their permanent income rather than their current income. At any moment a consumer may be earning more or less than their permanent income because of unexpected gains or losses (called positive or negative transitory income). Imagine you are given a one off bonus of £1000 - this is transitory income. Because you know it is a one off, it will have little impact on your overall earnings throughout your life and therefore your permanent income and so consumption is unlikely to change much. If, however, you knew you were going to inherit a significant sum of money in the future, you may take this into account and increase your estimate of your permanent income. This would increase consumption now, even though current income has not increased.

Life cycle hypothesis (Modigliani)
Households plan their expenditure over their life spans and aim to have fairly steady consumption. In your early years, for example, you will dissave because you have a low current income; during your mid-life you will save; and during retirement you will dissave. Consumption is related to your stage in the life cycle, not just current income.

Actual disposable income rises over an individual's lifetime until retirement, then falls to pension level. Consumption is spread equally over an individual's life

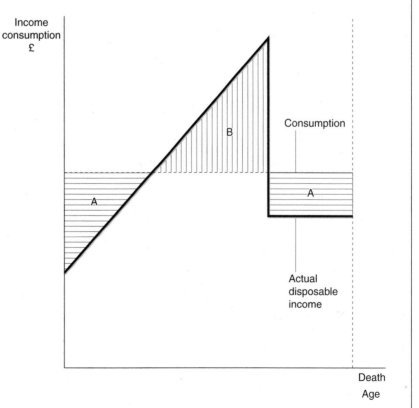

Area B is the amount the individual has to save to pay back (with interest) the borrowing in the early and late years (the two areas marked A)

Investment

Investment has two elements:
- the purchase of new capital, such as equipment and factories
- an increase in stock levels

Gross and net
Gross investment is the total level of investment
Net investment is the increase in the capital stock - some investment simply replaces capital which has worn out (i.e. depreciation)
Net Investment = Gross Investment – depreciation

Planned v. actual
Planned investment is the level of investment which firms intend to undertake at the beginning of the period. Actual investment is the level which has occurred at the end of the period. If firms fail to sell as much as they want to, they will be left with stocks which they had not planned for, i.e. actual investment will be greater than planned investment.

Autonomous and induced
- Autonomous investment is unrelated to the level of national income
- Induced investment is investment which is related to changes in the level of national income (see the accelerator)

Real v. Money investment
- 'Real' investment: investment in capital goods, e.g. factories, equipment, machinery
- Money investment: investment (savings) in 'paper', e.g. shares, bonds

The level of investment depends on
a) availability of finance
b) interest rates
c) the expected rates of return from the investment

The expected return from investment depends on, for example
- the initial cost of capital goods
- expected costs
- expected revenues
- expected productivity

If the expected rate of return is greater than the cost of borrowing (i.e. interest rates) the firm will invest. If the expected rate of return is less than the cost of borrowing, the firm will not invest.

Marginal efficiency of capital (MEC) shows rate of return on each additional unit of capital (Note: *technically the MEC shows the discount rate which equates the present value of a stream of expected inflows to its initial cost*)

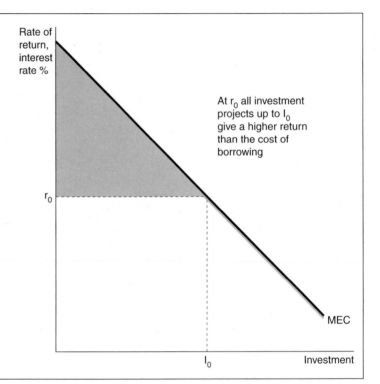

At r_0 all investment projects up to I_0 give a higher return than the cost of borrowing

Shifts in the investment schedule

Expectations are a key element of investment. Firms estimate costs and benefits for the future to determine the expected rate of return.

If expectations become more positive, e.g. the firm is more confident about the state of the economy and the level of demand for their product, then each project will be expected to have a higher rate of return; the MEC schedule will shift outwards.
The investment schedule can also shift because of
- a change in technology - this can increase productivity and make the projects more profitable
- lower taxation by the Government, increasing expected profits
- a fall in the purchase price of capital goods - this would increase the expected rate of return

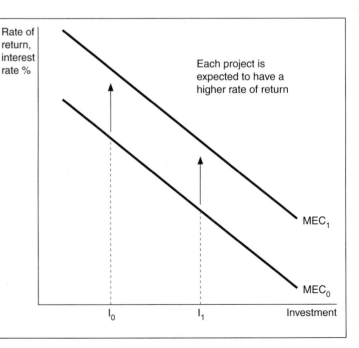

Each project is expected to have a higher rate of return

Investment continued

Movements along the investment schedule: changes in the interest rate

- with an increase in interest rates, investment is likely to fall. This is because it is more expensive to borrow and there are now less projects which have a higher rate of return than the cost of borrowing.
- with a fall in interest rates there are more projects which have a higher return than the cost of borrowing and investment should increase.

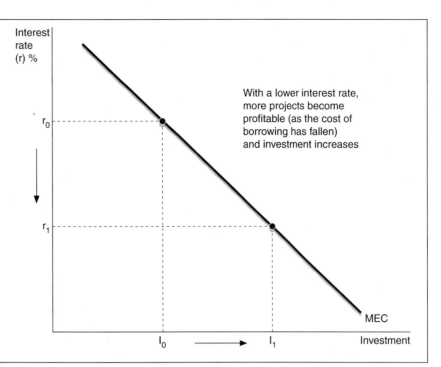

With a lower interest rate, more projects become profitable (as the cost of borrowing has fallen) and investment increases

---

Accelerator shows the relationship between net investment and the rate of change of national output.
The accelerator assumes a constant capital to output ratio, e.g. £2 of capital has to be purchased to be able to increase output by £1.

Desired output level (£)	Desired capital level (£)	Change in output (£)	Level of net investment (£)
200	400	–	–
220	440	+20	40
250	500	+30	60
300	600	+50	100
400	800	+100	200
600	1200	+200	400
700	1400	+100	200

Assume capital: output ratio of 2:1
- If output increases by an increasing (accelerating) amount firms will have to buy more machines each period, i.e. net investment will increase
- If output increases by a constant amount each period, firms will have to buy the same number of machines and factories; net investment will be constant
- If output increases but by less than the year before, firms will not need to buy as many machines and factories; net investment will actually fall.

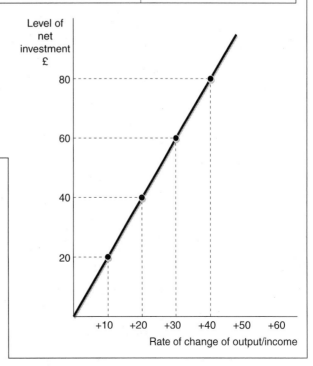

Limitations of the accelerator model
- firms often have stocks, so if output increases they can meet this without having to produce more
- the capital goods industry, which produces the capital goods, may not be able to increase supply, e.g. even if firms want to buy more machines they may not be able to
- with changes in technology, the accelerator coefficient may change and firms may not need to invest as much as before
- firms will have to be convinced the increase in demand is long term; otherwise they will be reluctant to invest - they may try to meet demand by using overtime

Investment continued

An increase in investment

- increases aggregate demand (and sets off the multiplier)
- can increase the growth of the economy
- increases capacity

The precise effect depends on the type of investment, e.g. whether it is in people, products or processes

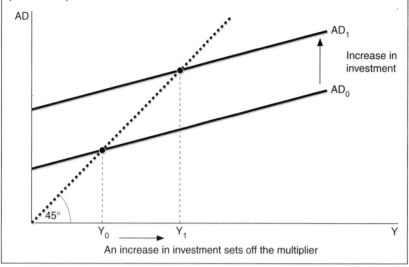

An increase in investment sets off the multiplier

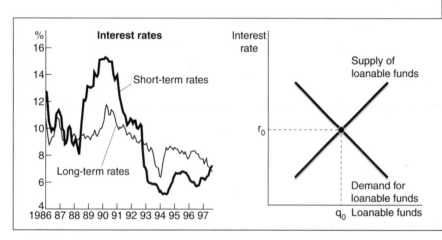

Interest

This is the return generated on capital and the cost of borrowing money. The interest paid for borrowing will depend on

- how long the loan is for - generally if you borrow for a longer time you are charged more
- risk - the riskier the project the more the lender will usually charge
- the cost of setting up the loan, i.e. it is cheaper to arrange one loan for £1mn than 100 loans of £10,000

What determines the interest rate?

a. The demand and supply of loanable funds.

Supply of loanable funds depends on

- people's willingness to save (and therefore provide funds which can be lent out)
- the ability of the banks to lend

Demand for loanable funds

- from households to buy consumer durables and non durables
- from firms for investment
- from the Government to finance their deficit

The demand is downward sloping because at higher rates of interest, households, firms, and the Government want to borrow less because it is more expensive to repay. Firms will find there are less projects which have a higher return than the cost of borrowing

b. The demand and supply of money *(see later)*

Real interest rates

means that they have been adjusted for inflation, e.g. if the nominal rate is 10% but inflation is 4% then in real terms the cost of borrowing is 6%.

Investment appraisal and present value

Discounted cash flow: technique of assessing investments

Firms estimate future expected revenues and costs and discount these to get their present value. £100 in 5 years time is not equal to £100 now - this is because money tends to grow over time due to interest rates. £60 now might become £100 in five years time, due to interest rates; and so the present value of £100 in five years time is £60 now. £100 has been discounted to £60. The higher the interest rate, the faster money grows over time and the lower the present value of any future income. Firms compare the present value of their expected earnings from a project with the supply price. If in today's terms the project is worth more than the initial cost, the firm will invest, i.e. if present value > supply price, invest. If the project in today's terms is worth less than the initial cost, do not invest, i.e. if the present value < supply price, do not invest. With a lower interest rate, the present value of future expected inflows increases and so more investment is likely to occur.

Higher interest rates

- make borrowing more expensive for households and firms, e.g. loans, credit cards, overdrafts, mortgages
- make savings more attractive (to earn higher returns)
- are likely to increase the external value of the pound due to more capital inflows and less capital outflows

Cost benefit analysis

This is an investment technique used by the Government, which takes into account external costs and benefits and attempts to value these. Used, for example, when deciding whether to build a motorway. The difficulty is deciding the money value of external effects.

Keynesian cross diagrams

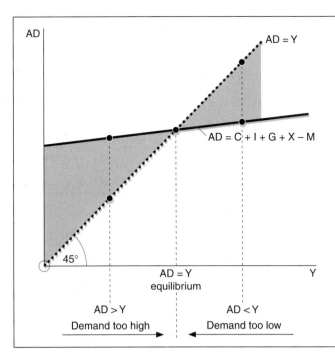

The 45 degree line shows all the combinations of points where the value of two axes are equal.

In this case the 45 degree line shows all the points at which the level of aggregate demand (AD) equals the level of output and income (Y), i.e. all the possible points of equilibrium where AD = Y i.e. aggregate demand = output

The economy will always move towards this point. If aggregate demand is greater than output there is an incentive for firms to produce more. If aggregate demand is less than output, there is an incentive for firms to produce less.
Note: in the Keynesian model, prices are assumed to be constant; i.e. firms change their output not their prices.
The aggregate demand schedule = C + I + G + X - M

The aggregate demand will shift upwards if there is:
- an increase in autonomous consumption
- an increase in investment (e.g. due to lower interest rates)
- an increase in Government spending (e.g. expansionist fiscal policy)
- an increase in exports (e.g. due to a lower exchange rate)
- a decrease in imports (e.g. due to quotas)

The slope of the aggregate demand depends on the marginal propensity to consume.

Aggregate demand

In a two sector economy, aggregate demand is made up of consumption by households and investment by firms.

Investment is drawn as a straight line on this diagram - it is assumed to be unrelated to the level of national income (i.e. exogenous or autonomous of income). Investment tends to be related to interest rates and expectations about the future level of income rather than the *present* income level in the economy.

In a three sector economy, aggregate demand is made up of consumption by households, investment by firms, and Government spending.

Government spending is drawn as a straight line in the diagram. This is because the level of Government spending depends on Government policy and not the level of income. The Government may or may not spend more in a boom or recession, we cannot definitely say, so we assume in this model that it is autonomous of national income.

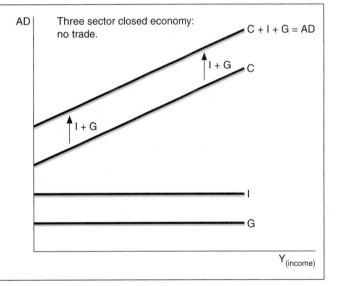

Inflationary gap

This occurs where the level of aggregate demand exceeds the level of output at full employment; this causes upward pressure on prices.

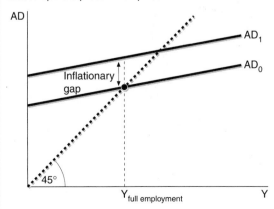

Deflationary gap

This occurs when the level of aggregate demand is below the level of output at full employment.

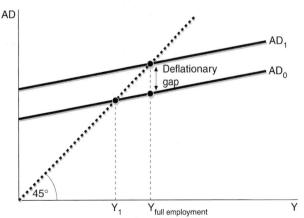

Keynesian cross diagrams continued

National income and the budget position

With an increase in national income, tax revenue will increase, e.g. more income tax, more VAT and less benefits. Assuming Government spending is autonomous, the budget position will move towards a surplus.

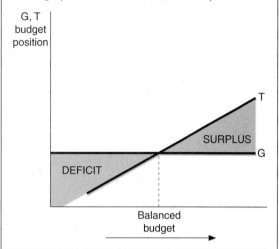

National income and the balance of trade

With an increase in income, more will be spent on imports. Assuming exports are autonomous, the balance of payments position worsens.

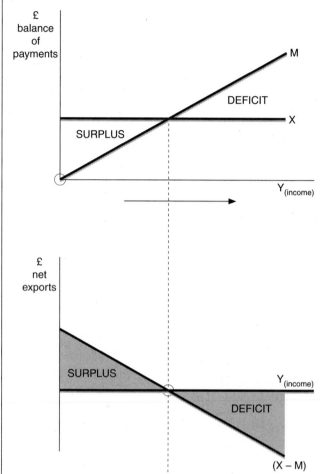

The multiplier

The multiplier shows how an increase in planned injections into the economy leads to a larger increase in output and income. This is because the initial injection sets off rounds of spending. It is based on the idea that 'one man's spending is another man's income'.
Imagine the Government spent £100m on building a new road. This £100m is paid to a building contractor who will spend some of this on buying equipment, materials, paying for labour, paying its overheads, and paying out to shareholders. For example, it may spend £80m. The rest is saved. The various groups which have received this money now go and spend some of this £80m. The shareholders might buy a holiday, the employees pay for their food, the suppliers pay their employees, and buy their materials. Of the £80m, £64m may be spent. This then becomes income for another set of people who again go and spend some of it.

The initial £100m creates a series of successively smaller increases in spending throughout the economy (in this case £100m + £80m + £64m +...)
The initial injection has a multiplied effect on the economy.
The size of the multiplier will depend on how much is spent at each stage, i.e. the marginal propensity to consume (mpc). The more that is spent at each stage (i.e. the larger the mpc) the bigger the overall effect.

$$\text{Multiplier} = \frac{\text{change in income}}{\text{change in injections}} = \frac{\Delta Y}{\Delta J}$$

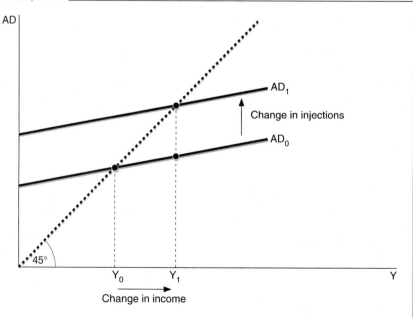

Keynesian cross diagrams continued

Size of the multiplier

The size of the multiplier can be calculated using the equation:

$$\frac{1}{1-mpc}$$

For example, if the mpc is 0.5, the multiplier is 2. If the mpc is 0.9, the multiplier is 10.

If the multiplier is 2, this means that any injection will have twice the effect on income, e.g. if the Government spends £100m this will lead to an increase of £200m in national income. If the multiplier is 10, this means any injection into the economy will have 10x the effect on national income, e.g. if the Government spends £100m this will lead to an increase of £1000m overall. The multiplier can also be expressed as

$$\frac{1}{mps + mpm + mrt}$$

Where mrt = marginal rate of tax = amount paid in tax out of each extra pound.

Mpm = marginal propensity to import = amount spent on imports out of each extra pound.

Mps = marginal rate of savings = amount saved out of each extra pound.

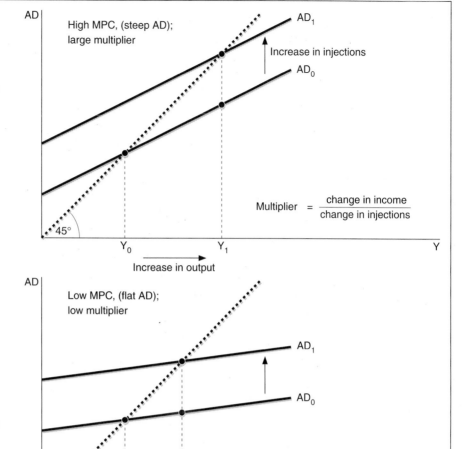

$$\text{Multiplier} = \frac{\text{change in income}}{\text{change in injections}}$$

Determinants of the size of the multiplier

- if the economy is open rather than closed, consumers will buy imports - this reduces the amount of money passed on at each stage of the multiplier process within the UK, i.e. it reduces their marginal propensity to consume within the UK so the multiplier is smaller
- interest rates - higher interest rates might encourage more saving and less spending and so reduce the multiplier
- tax rates - with higher tax rates, more of each pound is given to the Government and less is spent on UK goods and services; the multiplier is smaller

---

Marginal propensity to import depends on

- relative prices of UK and foreign goods - this will depend on the exchange rate to a large extent
- quality of goods and services
- income
- interest rates - if overseas rates are high, people in the UK will want to save abroad and money will leave the UK
- speculation - if people think the pound will fall, they will sell pounds now and buy foreign currency

Government policy and objectives

Objectives
- Stable prices, i.e. to keep inflation under control. This is important to keep UK firms competitive abroad and to help firms plan.
- Full employment, i.e. when all those willing and able to work at the given real wage are working. Unemployment is a waste of resources and means the economy is underproducing.
- Economic growth - this increases the standard of living.
- A balance of the balance of payments - a deficit means more money is leaving the country than is coming in; a surplus means another country has a deficit. A 'balance' may be desirable.

Priorities
These goals cannot necessarily be achieved at the same time. Policies taken to achieve one might disrupt others. More spending to increase employment levels, for example, may lead to higher inflation.

In the 1950s and 1960s the priority was usually full employment.

In the late 1970s, 1980s, and 1990s it was to control inflation.

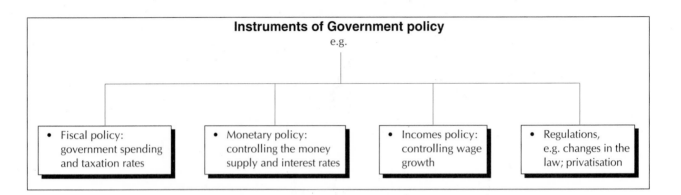

Instruments of Government policy
e.g.

- Fiscal policy: government spending and taxation rates
- Monetary policy: controlling the money supply and interest rates
- Incomes policy: controlling wage growth
- Regulations, e.g. changes in the law; privatisation

Types of policy

Demand side policies: attempts to influence aggregate demand

Supply side policies: attempts to influence aggregate supply

Reflationary policies: increasing aggregate demand, e.g. lower tax rates, higher Government spending, lower interest rates

Deflationary policies: decreasing aggregate demand, e.g. higher tax rates, lower Government spending, higher interest rates

Regional policies
Aim to reduce unemployment and increase the income of depressed regions or areas.
Interventionist policies:
- subsidies and tax concessions - these can be used to encourage firms into the area and to encourage firms to hire more people
- provision of facilities in depressed areas, e.g. better infrastructure (roads, communications etc.)
- taxation can be used to tax companies more in richer areas
- regulation - the Government can make it difficult for firms to expand in richer areas and easier to expand in poorer regions

Areas
- Assisted areas: areas which need Government assistance.

Funds
- Regional Selective Assistance involves discretionary grants for projects in assisted areas. To be given the grants, firms must prove they will create jobs.
- European Regional Development Fund - provides grants for job creating projects which develop the infrastructure.
- Regional Enterprise Grants - consist of innovation and investment grants.

Urban policy includes
- Enterprise zones - very small districts in urban areas. Major incentives are given to the firms setting up here, e.g. less bureaucracy, exemption from rates
- Training and Enterprise Councils - independent companies responsible for providing training in their regions.

Government policy and objectives continued

Privatisation

This involves transferring assets from the public sector to the private sector, e.g.

- contracting out - this is when activities undertaken by the public sector are sold off to the private sector, e.g. providing school meals, cleaning the roads

- deregulation - this is where regulations are changed or removed to allow more competition, e.g. bus services

- sale of assets, e.g. organisations such as British Gas have been sold to shareholders and are now privately owned

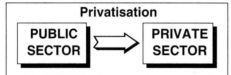

Privatisation

PUBLIC SECTOR → PRIVATE SECTOR

Examples of privatisation

British Aerospace 1981, British Gas 1986, British Airways 1987, British Steel 1989.

Why not privatise?

- may create private monopolies

- often sold very cheaply to make sure the shares are sold

Regulators

The government has set up watchdog bodies to monitor the privatised utility industries, e.g. Office of Gas Regulation (OFGAS); the Office for Telecommunication Regulation OFTEL. The utilities must meet the conditions of their operating licence which should ensure they do not abuse their market power. Prices are also controlled using a formula RPI - X; e.g. if X is set at 3% and inflation (RPI) is 4%, the utility can only increase prices by 1%.

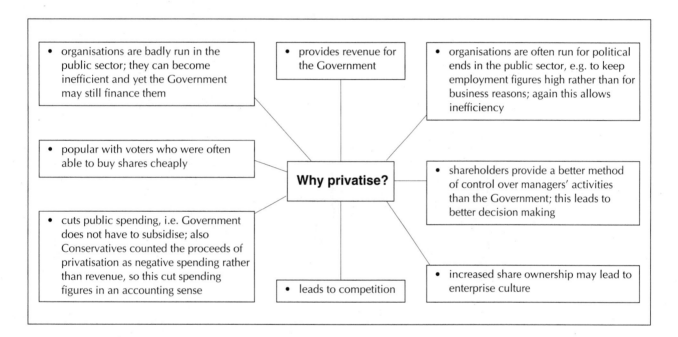

- organisations are badly run in the public sector; they can become inefficient and yet the Government may still finance them

- provides revenue for the Government

- organisations are often run for political ends in the public sector, e.g. to keep employment figures high rather than for business reasons; again this allows inefficiency

- popular with voters who were often able to buy shares cheaply

Why privatise?

- shareholders provide a better method of control over managers' activities than the Government; this leads to better decision making

- cuts public spending, i.e. Government does not have to subsidise; also Conservatives counted the proceeds of privatisation as negative spending rather than revenue, so this cut spending figures in an accounting sense

- leads to competition

- increased share ownership may lead to enterprise culture

Arguments against nationalisation

- lack of incentive - employees in the public sector lack the incentive to innovate

- firms may abuse their monopoly power

- firms may lack competitive pressure

Reasons for nationalisation

- large economies of scale - to have several companies producing in an industry with large economies of scale may lead to a duplication of resources

- externalities - by running an industry for itself, the Government can take account of negative and positive externalities, e.g. take account of social benefits

- capital spending - some industries may require high levels of expenditure; private firms may not be able to raise these funds

- prevents monopoly power by private firms

- strategic reasons, e.g. to keep control of an important industry such as defence

Fiscal policy

Involves the use of Government spending and taxation rates to control the economy.

Government spending includes

- health
- education
- law and order
- transport
- social security
- housing
- defence

General government expenditure 1995–96
Estimated outturn (Total expenditure excluding privatisation proceeds: £299.7bn)

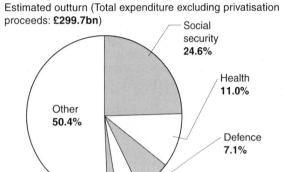

- Social security **24.6%**
- Health **11.0%**
- Other **50.4%**
- Defence **7.1%**
- Home office **2.2%**
- Education and employment **4.7%**

Revenue includes

- taxes
- privatisation proceeds
- rents from Government buildings and land
- profits of nationalised industries
- dividend income from any Government shares in private enterprises

Where the money comes from
Governments receipts **£308.4bn**, 1997–98

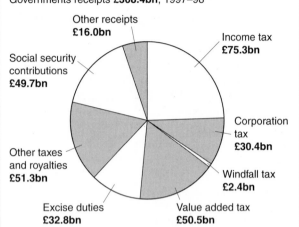

- Other receipts **£16.0bn**
- Income tax **£75.3bn**
- Social security contributions **£49.7bn**
- Corporation tax **£30.4bn**
- Other taxes and royalties **£51.3bn**
- Windfall tax **£2.4bn**
- Excise duties **£32.8bn**
- Value added tax **£50.5bn**

PSBR (Public Sector Borrowing Requirement)

- Total expenditure of central government, local government, nationalised industries, and other public sector bodies, minus tax revenue of central and local government, the revenue of nationalised industries and the fees from public corporations (e.g. BBC licence fees), i.e. PSBR = public sector spending - public sector receipts

PSBR	1990	1991	1992	1993	1994	1995
£m	–606	13757	36282	45418	35900	31745

Budget position

- Budget deficit: central government is spending more than it receives in tax revenue
- Budget surplus: central government spending is less than its tax revenue

PSDR (Public Sector Deficit Repayment)

When the public sector has a surplus (i.e. receipts are greater than spending) it can repay some of its debts.

Tax

Direct taxes: these take money directly from people's incomes or from companies' profits, e.g.

- income tax - payable on income
- corporation tax - paid by companies on their profits
- National insurance contributions - these are paid by individuals and are paid to the Department of Social Security.
- petroleum revenue tax which is charged on the net incomes of North Sea fields

Property taxes

- inheritance tax - paid when money is inherited
- capital gains tax - paid when an asset increases in value and is sold for more than it was bought for.
- council tax - this is a local tax paid by households and set by the local government in each area

Indirect taxes:

these are paid when goods and services are bought, e.g.

- Value Added Tax (VAT)
- tax on tobacco
- excise duties on alcohol

Tax systems

Total tax paid (vertical axis), Income (horizontal axis)

- Regressive Average tax rate rises
- Proportional Average tax rate is constant
- Progressive Average tax rate falls

(Note: to find the average tax rate on the diagram, measure the gradient of rays from the origin to different points on the curves)

- Proportional tax - as income rises, the proportion paid in tax stays constant, e.g. if people pay 15% on all their earnings
- Progressive tax - as income rises, the average rate of tax increases, i.e. people pay a greater proportion of their income in tax
- Regressive tax - as income rises, the average rate of income tax falls, i.e. people pay a smaller proportion of their income in tax

Fiscal policy continued

A good tax system should
- have horizontal equity - people in the same circumstances pay the same amount
- have vertical equity - taxes should be fair in terms of rich and poor
- be cheap to administer
- be difficult to evade; convenient to pay
- be easily understood by the taxpayer
- have limited disincentive effect, e.g. should not discourage people from working

Automatic stabilisers
If the income in the economy starts to grow, the progressive tax system acts as an automatic stabiliser. This is because more people will be paying a higher rate of tax, and so the level of disposable income and spending is less than it would be without a Government. This will dampen the effect of the boom. Similarly, the impact of a slump will be reduced because of transfer payments. When incomes fall, some people will become entitled to benefits which will keep their income and spending higher than it would be without a Government.
The tax system also reduces the size of the multiplier - out of each extra pound the consumer will have to pay some tax, so the marginal propensity to consume will fall. This reduces the multiplier, and so any change in injections will have a smaller effect.

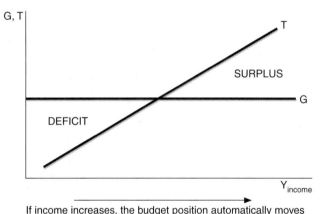

If income increases, the budget position automatically moves towards a surplus

Discretionary stabilisers
Actions deliberately taken by the Government to stabilise the economy, e.g. changes in the rate of taxation, spending on goods and services. In a slump, for example, the Government will usually try to reflate the economy by stimulating aggregate demand; in a boom it will try to deflate the economy by reducing aggregate demand.

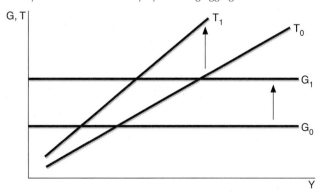

Discretionary changes in fiscal policy, e.g. an increase in tax rates or an increase in Government spending

---

Unemployment trap occurs when people are worse off by working than they are when they are receiving benefits. Because they lose benefits when they start work and are taxed on their income, their total income falls when they start work. This creates an incentive *not* to work.

Poverty trap occurs when people are worse off when they earn more! This is because some benefits are withdrawn.

Fiscal stance refers to whether the Government is pursuing an expansionist or contractionary policy, i.e. is the Government increasing or decreasing aggregate demand? To find this out, it is important to look at discretionary fiscal policy and ignore automatic effects of changing levels of income.

Reflationary fiscal policies include lower taxes and more Government spending. These increase aggregate demand.
Deflationary fiscal policies include higher taxes and less Government spending. These reduce aggregate demand.

Using tax changes compared to spending changes
Tax changes:
- tax and benefit changes can be introduced and have an effect quite quickly
- tax cuts can increase incentives (to work or to invest) and so have supply side effects

but
- they are an indirect method, i.e. the Government may not be able to predict how consumers will react to a tax cut - they may spend or save the extra money

Spending changes
- Government spending can be targeted at specific industries or regions
- this directly increases aggregate demand and so has full multiplier effects, e.g. £100 spending starts off the multiplier with a £100 increase in demand; if the Government gives £100 back in tax, some will be saved so the initial increase in demand will be lower

but
- there is a time lag before spending actually takes place, e.g. there may be long delay between deciding to increase spending and it actually occurring

---

Financing a deficit
To finance its deficit the Government can sell
- Treasury bills (short term borrowing by the Government) - these bills are IOUs which are bought back (redeemed) after three months
- Bonds - these are longer term debt, i.e. longer term IOUs
- National Savings certificates
  or
- The Bank of England can lend to the Government as the Government's banker

Fiscal policy continued

The impact of funding a deficit on the money supply

The existence of a deficit means that the Government is putting more money into the economy than it is taking out. This will increase the amount of money in the economy. If, however, the Government sells debt to the non bank public, or encourages people to use the National Savings, this will take the excess money out again, and the overall effect may be neutral. Similarly, if the Government sells long term debt to banks, this will reduce the banks' liquidity (because they have swapped cash for long term IOUs) and may reduce their lending. This might offset the increase in the money supply from the deficit. If the Government sells Treasury bills to banks, these are so liquid that it probably will not affect their lending - overall the money supply will have increased.

The National Debt

The National Debt is the total debt of the Government - it grows whenever the Government has a deficit because the Government is borrowing more money. The Government has to pay the interest of this borrowing back from future earnings.

- If the National Debt consists entirely of borrowings within the country, the Government is simply moving money around from one group to another. To pay off the people it owes interest to, it borrows from another group. When they have to be paid back, it borrows from another group. The money remains within the economy.
- If the Government borrows from overseas, the interest has to be paid to people out of the country and so the National Debt could become a burden.

Problems controlling spending

- some items of spending are very difficult to reduce, e.g. education and health spending - demand for these is ever increasing. People expect better standards and it is politically unwise to cut back on these.
- factors beyond the Government's control, e.g. an aging population, places a greater burden on the health service. Wars may require political intervention or more defence spending
- commitments to other countries or organisations such as the European Union are not easy to end

Problems of fiscal policy

- time lags - any change in policy will take time to work through the economy, by which time the policy change may not be needed
- information problems - it is difficult to know the exact position of the economy at any moment or to estimate the size of the multiplier or accelerator
- fiscal drag - if the Government keeps spending and taxation rates are constant, it will have a deflationary effect on the economy; as households and firms earn more, they move into higher tax brackets and pay more tax revenue to the Government.
- crowding out - the increase in income after an expansionist fiscal policy leads to more demand for money. Given the money supply, this increases interest rates which discourages private investment. The Government may boost demand, but the higher interest rates cause aggregate demand to fall again. The public sector 'crowds out' the private sector. Monetarists argue that the money demand is interest inelastic, so any shift in money demand will have a relatively large effect on interest rates. They also argue that investment is interest elastic, so any change in interest rates has a relatively large effect on investment and aggregate demand, and crowding out is a major problem.
- consumption may not be sensitive to tax changes, e.g. consumers may save any increase in disposable income rather than spending a proportion of it.
- Government intervention often overshoots or undershoots, i.e. increases aggregate demand too much or too little because of time lags and poor information; this can destabilise the economy.

Fine tuning/stabilisation policies

are attempts by the Government to use fiscal policy on a regular basis to increase or decrease aggregate demand, to keep it at a desired level to achieve its objectives. They were common in the 1950s and 1960s.

Fiscal policy v. monetary policy

Fiscal policy is likely to be more effective than monetary if
- money demand is interest elastic (so changes in the money supply have little effect on interest rates)
- the marginal efficiency of capital is interest inelastic (so interest rate changes have little effect on investment)

Fiscal policy post 1979

The Conservatives came to power in 1979 and believed
- fiscal policy was not effective at fine tuning the economy
- expansionist fiscal policy is inflationary
- there is a need to reduce Government spending, taxation, and borrowing as a percentage of national income
- monetary policy is more powerful

Keynesian fiscal policy

From the 1930s to the 1970s, governments tended to follow Keynesian policies on how to control the economy. This involved a belief that
- the economy will not necessarily be in equilibrium at full employment,

and that the Government needed to intervene to get it to full employment
- fiscal policy was effective
- by having a deficit, the Government can increase aggregate demand to achieve full employment
- fiscal policy can be used to fine tune the economy to stabilise growth

Balanced budget multiplier (equal to 1)

An increase in Government spending accompanied by an equal increase in tax revenue leads to an increase in output. For example, if Government spending increases by £100, and at the same time the Government raises an extra £100 in tax, there will still be a multiplied effect on the economy. Out of every £100 given to households, some is spent and some is saved, e.g. £80 spent and £20 saved. Therefore, if tax revenue is increased by £100, the impact on spending is a fall of only £80 (the rest comes from saving). As a result, if Government spending goes up by £100, aggregate demand rises by £100, but if taxation rises by £100 aggregate demand initially falls by only £80. The overall result is a £20 increase in demand, which sets off the multiplier even though the budget is balanced. The balanced budget multiplier is equal to 1. In this case the multiplier will be 5 (MPC = 0.8); so the overall effect is £20 x 5= £100 which is equal to the initial injection.

Money and banking

The functions of money:
- medium of exchange - people are willing to change their goods and services for money
- a store of value - people are willing to hold on to money because it generally keeps its value (although not with inflation)
- unit of account - people can measure the value of things in terms of money
- standard of deferred payment - people are willing to accept money as payment in the future, e.g. when the work is completed

Financial institutions

- Discount houses. There are only eight discount houses in the UK. They act as intermediaries between the Bank of England and the commercial banks, and specialize in very short term borrowing and lending. They borrow money from the commercial banks for short periods of time (this is known as money at call) and lend short term bills from the Bank of England (Treasury bills).

- foreign banks

- Building societies. These used to specialize in loans to people to buy houses, but increasingly they are competing directly with the banks. Many building societies have actually become banks in recent years, e.g. Abbey National.

- Finance houses. These finance hire purchase agreements, e.g. when you buy a TV or computer you often arrange to pay the money over several months or years. This is done by borrowing from a finance house.

- Commercial banks. Known as retail banks, e.g. Barclays, National Westminster, and Lloyds. They are owned by shareholders. They aim to attract savings from customers which are then lent out to other customers or invested. They specialize in providing banking services to individuals.

- Merchant banks, e.g. Rothschilds. These banks specialize in advising large companies on raising money and are involved in issuing shares for them (which means they are acting as an issuing house). They are also accepting houses, which means that for a fee they guarantee payment on bills of exchange (bills of exchange are IOUs).

Functions of the Bank of England

- Banker to the Government - provides an account for the Government. Manages the National Debt by arranging the sale of bonds. Redeems (buys back) debt when it has matured. Pays interest for the Government onto debt and actually holds debt itself.

- Controls the country's currency - sole power to issue bank notes in England. Note: the actual number of notes and coins is determined by how much people want to hold in bank deposits or as cash.

- supports financial institutions - acts as lender of last resort, i.e. will lend to the financial institutions if necessary.

- Agent for the Government's exchange rate policy - holds the official currency reserves and will buy and sell currency for the Government.

- Banker to retail banks - holds deposits of retail banks and will lend funds to them.

- Oversees the financial system - licenses deposit takers in the UK; regulates various financial services.

Departments of the Bank of England

Issue department - responsible for issuing notes and coins
Banking department - acts as banker to the Government and retail banks

In May 1997, the UK Chancellor of the Exchequer announced several changes which made the Bank of England more independent from Government pressure. Interest rates are now set by the Bank's Monetary Policy Committee (MPC), which uses its own judgment about an appropriate level to control inflation. The operational target for the MPC in 1997 was for an underlying inflation (RPI excluding mortgage interest payments, called RPIX) of 2.5%. MPC sets interest rates with reference to inflation two year's ahead.

Credit creation and the money multiplier

When money is deposited in a bank, some is kept in reserve and the rest is lent out; this increases the money supply and is known as 'credit creation'.
If r is the reserve ratio (i.e. the percentage of deposits kept in reserve) the effect of an initial deposit is an increase of $(1 \div r) \times$ the initial deposit.

E.g. r = 0.1 (i.e. the banks keep 10% in reserve)
initial deposit = £20
Overall impact = $(1 \div 0.1) \times 20 = £200$ i.e. with an initial deposit of £20, overall deposits will increase to £200.

Money and banking continued

Measures of the money supply

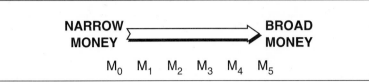

NARROW MONEY → BROAD MONEY

M_0 M_1 M_2 M_3 M_4 M_5

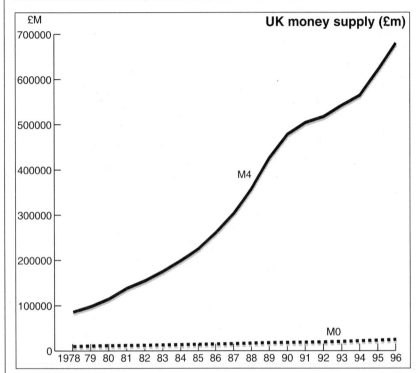

UK money supply (£m)

M5 – M4 plus other holdings of liquid assets, e.g. bills of exchange eligible for rediscount at the Bank of England, short term loans to local authorities, short and medium term deposits in the National Savings Bank and certificates of tax deposit

Note:

- *sight deposits – deposits at banks which can be withdrawn without notice*
- *time deposits – bank accounts which require a minimum period of notice*
- *retail deposits – this refers to deposits of the general public at banks and building societies which can be used for transactions purposes*
- *wholesale deposits – normally held by banks and financial institutions in other banks and financial institutions*

The existence of different definitions highlights the problem of controlling the money supply, i.e. there are many views of what the money supply actually is. If you control one definition you do not necessarily control another, e.g. if you control sight deposits, people might simply move to time deposits

In the UK, the Government stopped publishing targets for broad money (e.g. M3) after 1986 although it still monitored its growth. As building society deposits became more liquid, M2 and M4 became the main measures of narrow and broad money rather than M1 and M3.

M0 (narrowest definition of money) – notes and coins (in tills and in banks' tills) and operational balances that banks hold with the Bank of England. This is a measure of the 'monetary base'.

M1 – notes and coins in circulation and sterling private sector sight deposits

This measure was dropped in 1989

NIBM1 (Non interest bearing M1) – excludes all sight deposits which pay interest

M2 – NIBM1 plus all other retail deposits in banks and building societies

M3 – M1 plus all sterling private sector time deposits in banks plus private sector holdings of bank certificates of deposit

M3c – M3 plus private sector holdings of foreign currency bank deposits

M4 – M3 plus private sector holdings of building society shares and deposits and sterling certificates of deposits

M4c – includes sterling and foreign currency private sector deposits in banks and building societies

M3H – includes public corporations' holdings of money

Broad Money supply
M4, Annual percentage changes

Money and banking continued

Instruments and objectives of monetary policy

- Objectives - what the authorities are trying to achieve

- Instruments - what they are using to achieve their objectives

The objective of monetary policy is usually to control.
In the early 1980s, the Government tried to achieve this by controlling banks' lending.
From the mid 1980s, the Government has used the interest rate as the main policy instrument; this is aimed at controlling demand for money rather than supply.

Monetary and inflation targets

These were introduced by the Government in the early 1980s as part of its Medium Term Financial Strategy. By achieving these, the Government hoped to control the growth of the money supply and control inflation. By announcing money supply targets, they hoped people would believe that inflation would be reduced and so reduce their own wage demands in line. In fact the Government generally missed its targets. The Government now publishes inflation targets.

Controlling the money supply

- open market operations - the Bank of England sells Government debt (short term debt is called Treasury bills; longer term debt is called bonds). The buyer pays for these by writing a cheque on their banks. The banks honour the cheque by paying the Bank of England and this reduces their reserves and so reduces their ability to lend.

- liquidity (or reserve) ratios - by forcing a bank to keep more funds in reserve, a central bank can restrict the commercial banks' lending; but banks may find ways around this, e.g. Goodhart's Law (if the Bank of England tries to control one type of lending, banks will find ways of increasing other types).

- cut the PSBR - the PSBR increases the money supply if it is financed by selling Treasury bills or borrowing from the Bank of England; but cutting the PSBR may be difficult as it involves cutting public spending and increasing taxes.

- funding - this involves converting short term Government debt to long term debt. By selling longer term debt to banks in return for shorter term debt, the central bank reduces their liquidity and ability to lend. In the mid 1980s the Government undertook 'overfunding', where the value of the bonds sold is in excess of the PSBR.

- special directives and special deposits - banks can be forced to deposit a certain percentage of their liabilities with the Bank of England, e.g. in the 1970s the authorities used Special Supplementary Deposits (The Corset). Banks had to put a proportion of their deposits at the Bank of England without interest. The Bank of England can also give directives on how much banks are allowed to lend (quantitative controls) or who to (qualitative controls). These types of control have not been used in the UK since the 1970s.

- moral suasion - the central bank can make it known whether it would like more or less lending; banks will often listen to the central bank's advice or wishes

Problems of monetary control

- banks may hold in excess of the reserve set by the authorities, so a reserve ratio or special deposits may have no impact.

- Goodhart's Law - attempts to control particular types of lending or lending by certain financial institutions will lead to more lending of a different type or by different organisations.

- disintermediation lending continues, but banks are no longer the intermediaries, i.e. it is no longer officially organised by banks and so the authorities cannot control it.

Controlling interest rates

Open market operations are often conducted to leave the banks short of cash. The banks then borrow this, which often means they are competing for scarce funds which will make it more expensive to borrow, i.e. increase interest rates. The Bank of England can also change the interest rate by changing its discount rate - this is the rate at which it buys bills. By influencing the interest rate, the Bank of England influences the demand for money.

Problems of using interest rates

Changes in interest rates are likely to affect

- the exchange rate, e.g. using higher interest rates to discourage borrowing may increase the value of the exchange rate and make UK firms uncompetitive

- borrowing by households and firms

Also, they may take time to have an effect

The demand for money (liquidity preference)

People can hold money or they can hold other assets such as houses or bonds (IOUs). According to Keynes, people hold money for three main reasons:

* Transactions demand - money is needed to facilitate transactions, i.e. to buy goods and services. This will increase if

a) we have more income (because we will buy more goods and services)

b) prices increase (because we will need more money to buy our goods and services)

c) if we are paid less regularly

Assume the household receives £2000 every 4 weeks and uses this up at a constant rate.
Average holdings will be £1000

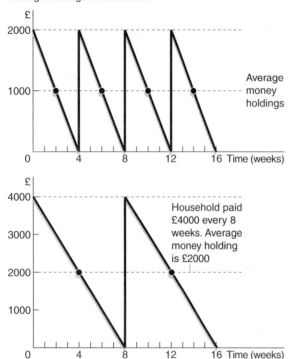

* Precautionary demand - this money is held in case of emergency, e.g. people might hold money in case they lose their job. This demand will usually rise with income.
* Speculative demand – this is money which is held rather than investing it in bonds or other assets. If people think the price of other assets is going to fall they will switch to money.

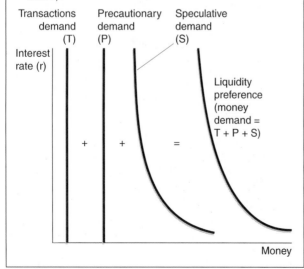

The transactions and precautionary demand for money are called demand for 'active balances', i.e. there is an active reason for holding money.

The speculative demand is called an 'idle balance' - money is held because the individual is worried about holding bonds.

Speculative demand and interest rates
Money is liquid but it does not earn a rate of return. If people are holding money, they are not earning interest. The interest rate represents the opportunity cost (or price) of holding money. If the interest rate is high, this will reduce the desire to hold money. If the interest rate is low there will be less incentive to switch out of money into other assets.

The money market and the bond market
A bond has a fixed return, e.g. £10 a year. If the price of a bond is £100 this represents a 10% return. If the price of the bond is £50 this represent a 20% return, i.e. the lower the price of the bond, the greater the return.

If households and firms feel they have too much liquidity, i.e. they are holding too much money, they will want to switch into bonds. This will increase the price of bonds (and so lower their return). This process will continue until the price of bonds has increased (the rate of return on bonds has fallen) to a point where there is no further desire to switch away from money, i.e. both the money market and bonds markets are back in equilibrium.

At interest rates above r_0 there is excess supply of money; households buy bonds until equilibrium r_0

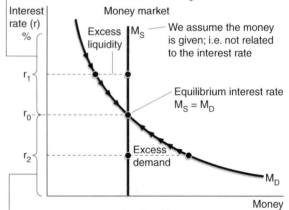

At interest rates below r_0 there is excess demand for money; households sell bonds leading to a fall in their price and increase in interest rates until there is no further incentive to sell at r_0

Keynesians and monetarists and the demand for money
Keynesians see money as an alternative to bonds and financial assets. Monetarists believe money is an alternative to a broader range of alternatives, including physical goods. Any excess liquidity will lead to a direct increase in spending on goods, as well as switching into financial assets, according to the monetarists. However, monetarists also believe that money is NOT a close substitute for other assets and, therefore, changes in the interest rate have relatively little effect, i.e. money demand is interest inelastic.

The monetary transmission mechanism

This shows how changes in money supply or demand can influence the level of national income.

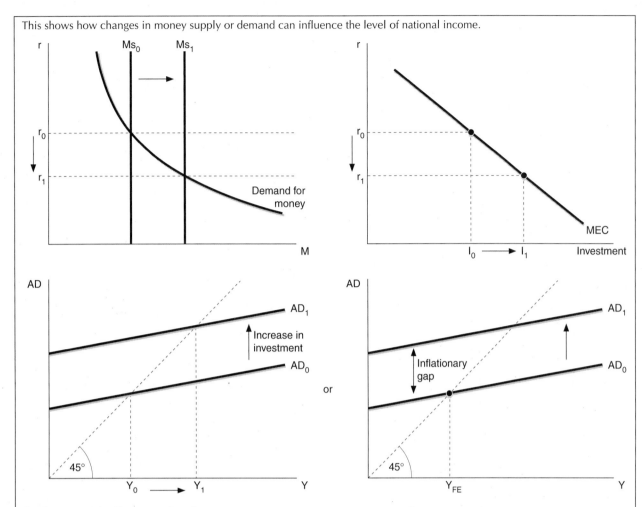

An increase in the supply of money

- **Money market**

  Imagine there is an increase in the money supply. At the old level of interest rates there is now excess liquidity, i.e. too much money. Households try to shed this liquidity by moving out of money into bonds and other assets. This bids up the price of bonds (and so reduces their return - the interest rate). This process continues until bond prices are so high (interest rates so low) that there is no further incentive to move out of money. Both the money and the bond markets are back in equilibrium.

- **The capital goods market**

  The lower interest rate will increase the amount of investment - because the cost of borrowing has fallen, there are more investment projects which are now profitable. The extent of the increase in investment will depend on how sensitive investment is in relation to changes in the interest rate, i.e. the interest rate elasticity of investment.

- **The goods market**

  With an increase in investment, there is an increase in aggregate demand.
  If the economy is below full employment, this will lead to an increase in output and employment.
  If the economy is at full employment, this will lead to an inflationary gap and upward pressure on prices.

  If prices do increase, this will increase the money value of national income, which will increase the transactions demand for money. This will shift the demand for money outwards which in turn increases interest rates and brings aggregate demand down again, i.e. a one off increase in the money supply will create forces that reduce any inflationary gap and so the inflation. This assumes that the money supply is held constant and not increased again. If the money supply is increased at the same rate as prices are increasing, inflation can continue.

An increase in the demand for money

- **Money market**

  At the old interest rate there is now excess demand for money. Households will switch out of assets into money, i.e. they will sell their bonds. This reduces the price of the bonds and increases their rate of return (the interest rate) This process continues until there is no further incentive to move out of bonds.

- **Capital goods market**

  The higher interest rate should lead to a fall in investment, depending on the interest elasticity of investment.

- **The goods market**

  With a fall in investment there will be a fall in the level of aggregate demand.

The monetary transmission mechanism continued

Monetarists and the transmission mechanism

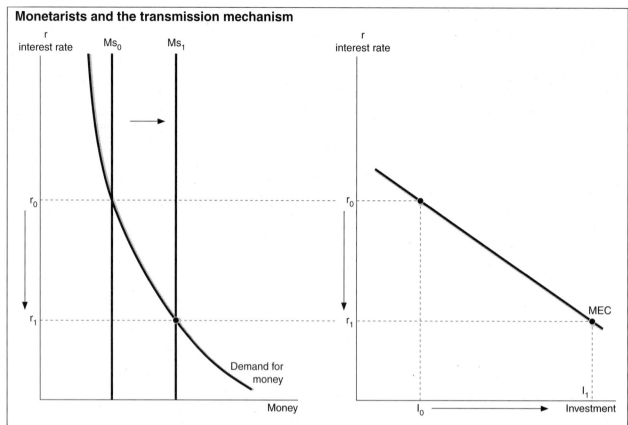

Monetarists believe
- the link between money supply and aggregate demand is not only indirect through interest rates and investment, but also direct - i.e. given excess liquidity, households and firms spend more on goods and services.
- lower interest rates increase households' consumption as well as investment by firms

- demand for money is interest inelastic, so any increase in the money supply leads to a large fall in interest rates and a large effect on aggregate demand
- investment is interest elastic, so any change in interest rates has a significant effect on aggregate demand

- investment is not vulnerable to changes in expectations and so a fall in interest rates will increase aggregate demand
i.e. monetarists believe the link between money and aggregate demand is very strong. Because they believe the economy is at/near full employment, an increase in aggregate demand will lead to inflation.

Liquidity trap occurs when an increase in the money supply does not affect the interest rate (and so does not affect investment or aggregate demand).

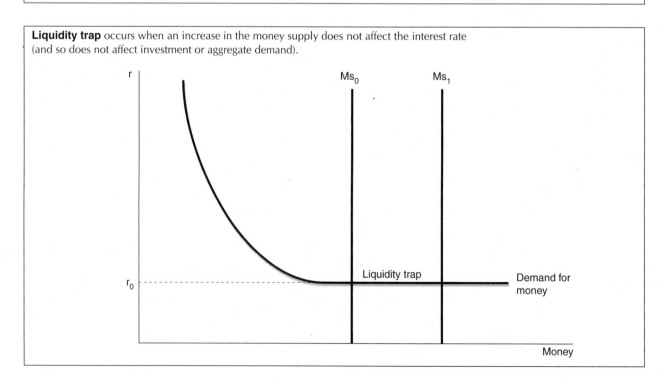

Inflation

This is a sustained increase in the general price level. It is usually measured by the Retail Price Index (RPI). This is a weighted average of retail prices. To calculate it, goods and services are given different weights according to the percentage of income that households spend on them. Weights are determined by results of the Family Expenditure Survey.

Inflation can be caused by
- too much demand in the economy. This is called demand-pull inflation, e.g. the UK in the 1980s. If demand increases and firms cannot produce enough output, they will increase their prices.
- higher costs forcing firms to increase their prices. This is called cost-push inflation, e.g. as happened in Western Europe in the 1970s when oil prices increased.
- excessive growth of the money supply

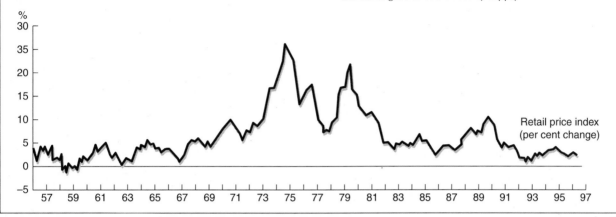

Types of inflation
- creeping inflation - slowly increasing rates of inflation, e.g from 5 to 6%
- strato-inflation - fairly high inflation, e.g. 10 to several hundred %
- hyperinflation - extremely high rates of inflation, e.g. thousands of %

Causes of demand pull inflation
- reflationary policies by the Government
- increased consumer spending, e.g. through greater consumer confidence

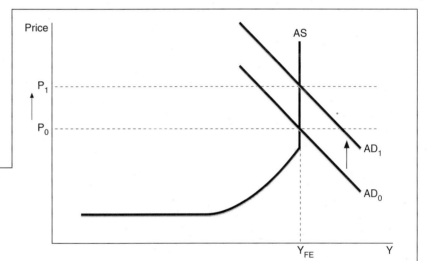

Causes of cost push inflation
- wage increases to employees which are not linked to higher productivity
- an increase in the cost of imported raw materials, e.g. because of a fall in the value of the pound
- an increase in input prices, e.g. because of the monopoly power of suppliers

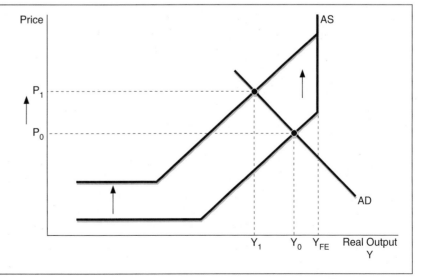

Inflation continued

Wage price spiral

Higher wage demands without any increase in productivity lead to higher costs and then prices (cost push inflation); higher prices lead to higher wage demands.

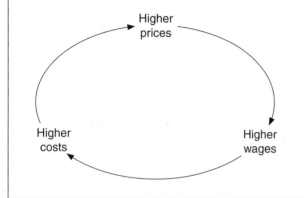

Fisher equation of exchange

MV = PY

where

M = quantity of money, i.e. the supply of money

V = the income velocity of circulation, i.e. the average number of times per year that the typical unit of money must be spent to buy the goods and services bought that year

P = average level of all prices

Y = number of transactions of final products

This is not an equation, it is an identity, i.e. it must be true. MV represents total spending in an economy; PY represents the total amount of money received for the goods and services, i.e. money national income. They show the same things. For example, if there is £100bn in the economy, which is spent 5 times, then total spending must be £500bn. This must equal the value of the money received for goods and services (i.e. £500bn)

Using MV = PY

If the number of transactions is 200 and the average price level is £20, then the total spent must be 200 × £20, i.e. £4000.

If the total money in the economy is £400, then each pound must have been used 10 times, i.e. the velocity is 10.

The quantity theory of money

The quantity theory of money states that the price level is directly related to the amount of money in the economy. Using MV = PY, we can see this is true if V and Y are constant, i.e. if V and Y are fixed, then the price level is directly proportional to the money supply.

Imagine V = 10 and Y = 30

If the money supply is £60 then prices will be £20; (£60 × 10 = £20 × 30)

If the money supply doubles to £120 and V and Y do not change, then prices increase to £40 (120 × 10 = £40 x 30), i.e. the price level depends on the money supply

Why should V and Y be constant?

- V may be constant because the rate at which money is spent may not change very much over time.
- Y may be constant if the economy is near full employment, which would mean that the output and, therefore, number of transactions in the economy could not change much.

Quantity theory of money and monetarists

Monetarists believe in the quantity theory of money. According to monetarists, the price level is directly related to the money supply.

To control prices (and so inflation) the Government should control the money supply.

Keynesians and the Fisher equation of exchange

Keynesians believe

- the velocity of circulation can change - with more money people may hold on to it (V falls)
- an increase in the money supply can lead to more output (Y) rather than higher prices

Is inflation a monetary phenomenon?

According to monetarists, inflation is 'always and everywhere a monetary phenomenon'. Temporary bursts of inflation may be caused by, for example, costs rising, but if prices are to rise continuously, the money supply must also be increased.

- redistribution of income - some groups whose earnings are too linked to inflation will find their real earnings fall (e.g. employees with weak bargaining power, such as shop assistants); also borrowers may gain whilst lenders lose unless loans are index linked (i.e. linked to inflation)

- planning difficulties - firms may delay investment if they are unsure of the price they will buy inputs at or sell their goods at

- uncompetitiveness abroad (assuming UK inflation is higher than overseas and the exchange rate does not fall to compensate)

Problems of inflation

- shoe leather costs - with inflation, households and firms will have to search for good returns from their savings to protect their real earnings. This involves extra costs called 'shoe leather' costs

- menu costs, e.g. the costs of changing the prices in publicity material, displays, and slot machines

Inflation continued

Curing inflation

The cure depends on the cause, i.e. what type of inflation it is. Policies include:
- demand side policies - reduce aggregate demand, e.g. reduce public expenditure, raise taxes, increase interest rates
- supply side policies - to make the labour market more competitive (e.g. reduce trade union power, cut unemployment benefits) or to increase competition (e.g. privatisation, encourage small firms and business start ups)
- prices and incomes policies
- exchange rate policy, e.g. increase value of the currency to reduce import prices and reduce demand for exports

Prices and incomes policies

These are attempts by the Government to control the increase in prices and/or incomes by legislation.

Problems of incomes policies:
- once the legal restrictions are ended, people often try to catch up on the money they did not get before, i.e. there is a surge in wages and prices
- they prevent the market system working, e.g. firms cannot attract the labour they want through higher wages
- they are politically unpopular and can cause industrial relations problems
- firms find ways of avoiding the policy. This is called wage drift - although the wage per hour stays constant, the unit cost of production increases because firms find ways of paying more, e.g. extra benefits (such as cars or cheap borrowing), extra payments for overtime which is not actually worked, or extra holiday pay.

Multi-causal inflation

In reality, inflation is likely to be due to a variety of causes not just one.

Inflation reduces the purchasing power of a pound

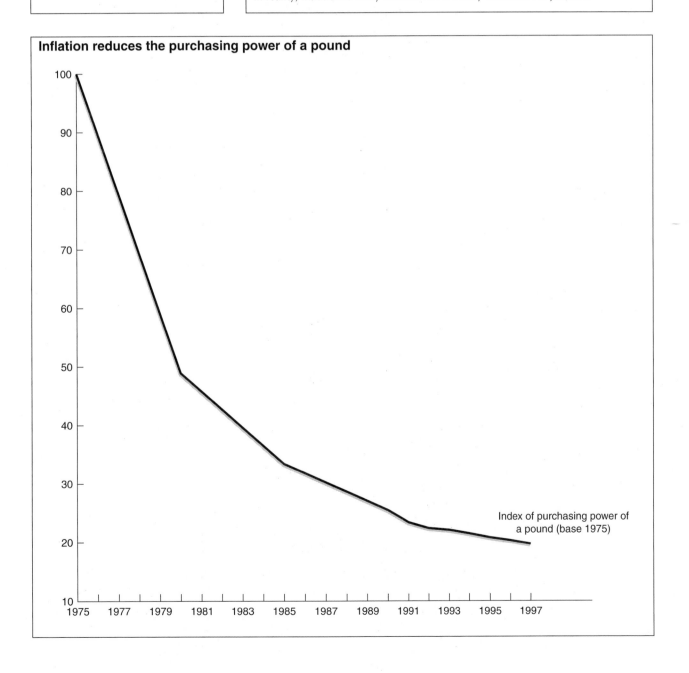

Index of purchasing power of a pound (base 1975)

Unemployment

- Unemployed - those who are not employed but who want a job
- The labour force - those in a job plus those who are unemployed

1997 labour force statistics

Total workforce	28.16m
Total in employment	26.16m (of which self employment = 3.25m)
Unemployment	2.0m (of which short term unemployment = 1.31m)
Non participants	18.55 m

UK measure of unemployment - those who are in receipt of unemployment benefit and who are available to undertake any suitable work. This definition excludes groups such as school-leavers and men over 60 who are unemployed but not in receipt of unemployment benefit

- Regional - unemployment associated with particular regions of the country; often due to structural unemployment

- Real wage (or classical) - unemployment caused by real wages being too high, e.g. because of union power

- Structural - people who are unemployed because of changes in the nature of the economy, e.g. due to the decline of traditional manufacturing industries

- Cyclical (or Keynesian) - unemployment associated with a slump or downturn in economic activity

Types of unemployment

- Seasonal - people who are unemployed because of the season, e.g. fruit pickers in the winter

- Frictional - people who are between jobs

Voluntary and involuntary

- 'Voluntary' unemployment occurs when all those willing and able to work at the given real wage rate are working, i.e. the economy is at full employment. Even at full employment some people will still be unemployed, e.g. due to frictional causes.
- 'Involuntary' unemployment occurs when people are willing and able to work at the given real wage rate but no job is available, i.e. the economy is below full employment. A worker is 'involuntarily' unemployed if he or she would accept a job at the given real wage.

Natural rate of unemployment, or the NAIRU (non accelerating rate of unemployment)

This is the rate of unemployment when inflation is correctly anticipated. This level of unemployment occurs when the economy is at full employment; i.e. when the labour market is in equilibrium.

The level of the natural rate of unemployment depends on the supply side of the labour market, e.g. training, information, benefit levels, unions

Full employment occurs when all those willing and able to work at the given real wage are working, i.e. all unemployment is 'voluntary'.

Is all unemployment 'voluntary' at full employment?

Arguably yes, for example

- Frictional is 'voluntary' because people have decided to look for another job.
- Seasonal is 'voluntary' because people have decided to take a job in which they are only seasonally employed; they could take other work in the 'off' season
- Real wage is 'voluntary' because workers or their unions have decided to push up wages and have 'volunteered' some workers for unemployment
- Structural may be regarded as 'voluntary' if workers who have left a job in a declining industry are unwilling to accept a job at a lower wage rate in another industry.

The word 'voluntary' does not mean people actually volunteer to be unemployed.

Unemployment continued

Monetarist and Keynesian views of unemployment

Monetarists believe that money wages and prices are flexible and adjust quickly, so that the real wage is at the right level to achieve long run equilibrium in the labour market, i.e. the labour market clears quickly and is either at or approaching full employment; all unemployment is 'voluntary'.

Keynesians believe money wages are slow to adjust (e.g. due to money illusion, fixed contracts or because employers and employees want long run money wage stability), and so the real wage may not adjust to clear the labour market, i.e. there can be 'involuntary' and 'voluntary' unemployment.

Imagine demand falls and inflation falls. If money wages fall as well, the real wage remains unchanged and the economy stays at full employment (monetarist). If money wages do not fall, the real wage has increased and there will be less labour demanded and there will be 'involuntary' unemployment in the short run until money wages do fall (Keynesian). The problem according to Keynesians is that the 'short run' can actually be quite a long time, which is why the Government should intervene.

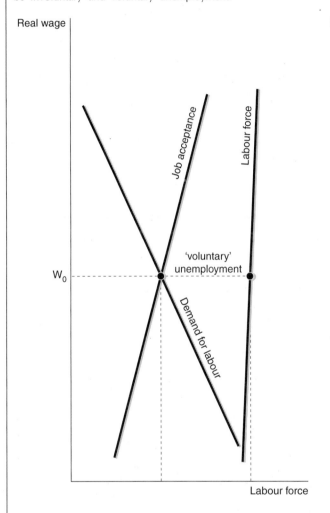

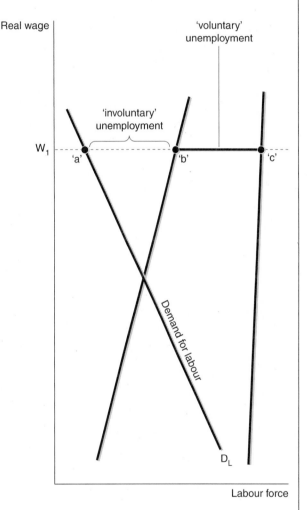

Job acceptance = number of workers willing and able to accept a job at each real wage. As the real wage increases, so does the number of people willing to accept jobs.

Labour force = number of people registered for work; this will also increase at higher real wages as people come back into the labour force.

The difference between the number of people in the labour force and the number accepting a job is 'voluntary unemployment'.

At real wage w_1 there are 'c' people in the labour force; 'b' want to accept a job, so 'bc' is 'voluntary' unemployment; 'ab' is 'involuntary' unemployment - these people are willing and able to work but are not demanded at the higher real wage.

This assumes the high real wage is caused by imperfections in the labour market, e.g. money illusion which prevents money wages changing quickly.

If the real wage is above equilibrium because of union power, it could be argued that 'ab' is 'voluntary' - the unions have volunteered workers for unemployment. This is 'classical unemployment'.

Unemployment continued

Why does unemployment matter?
- it is a waste of resources so the economy is underproducing compared to its potential output; it is inefficient
- it can cause social problems, e.g. higher crime rates
- the Government loses tax revenue, e.g. less income tax as less people are working and less VAT as there is less spending

Employment trends in the UK

Deindustrialisation - decline in the manufacturing sector

Growth of employment in services
- high income elasticity of demand for services making this a growth sector as the economy grows
- UK comparative advantage in this sector
- import penetration less easy in the service sector

Decline in employment in manufacturing in the 1980s
- high exchange rates in the early 1980s made UK manufacturers uncompetitive
- high interest rates made expansion expensive
- technological change replaced some manual jobs
- inefficiency - a need to reduce overmanning and improve working practices
- the structural decline of certain industries, e.g. coal
- greater competition from abroad

Growth of self employment
- high redundancies in the early 1980s - many used redundancy money to start up for themselves
- Government advice and incentives
- inspired by success of others

UK unemployment rate

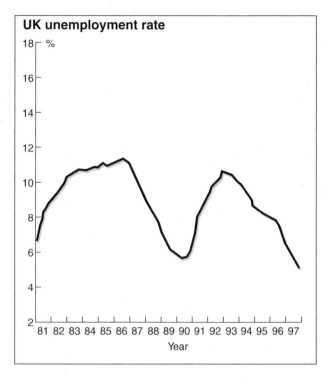

Cures for unemployment

To cure 'involuntary' unemployment, the Government can stimulate demand to provide more jobs, i.e. use demand side policies.
To cure 'voluntary' unemployment, the Government has to make more people willing and able to work. This can be done via supply side policies, e.g.
- more training to give people the necessary skills
- a reduction in income tax so the gains of working compared to collecting benefit are greater

- a reduction in unemployment benefits to give people more incentive to look for work
- more information about vacancies and help with applications
- help (e.g. financial) for people who are relocating
- reduce barriers to people accepting jobs, e.g. there used to be 'closed shops' which were factories where only union members could work; this prevented non union members working

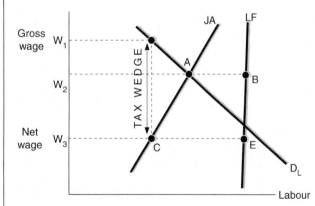

The effect of an income tax cut

With income tax there is a differnce between the gross wage paid by the firm and the net wage received by the worker e.g. $W_1 W_3$. At W_3 the natural rate of unemployment is CE; C people want to work at this wage but there are E people in the labour force. If income taxes are removed, the gross and net wage are the same at W_2 and the level of 'voluntary' unemployment falls to AB.

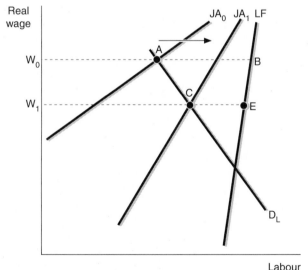

Policies aimed at making people more willing or able to work, shift the job acceptance to the right. 'Voluntary' unemployment falls from AB to CE.

The Phillips curve

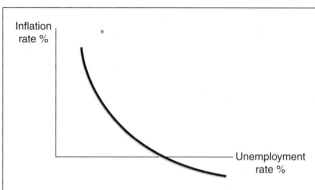

The Phillips curve shows the relationship between inflation and unemployment.
(Note: the original curve showed the relationship between the rate of change of nominal wages and unemployment, NOT the rate of change of prices and unemployment)
The curve was originally produced by A W Phillips in 1958, and suggested a trade off between inflation and

unemployment, i.e. if unemployment fell, inflation would rise and vice versa. This fitted in with thinking at the time, i.e. to reduce inflation the Government had to spend more money to boost aggregate demand, and this would probably cause some inflation; the higher levels of demand would pull up prices. Workers would become more confident because the economy was doing well and because it was not as easy for employers to find new employees, and so wages would be pushed up causing cost push inflation. The model suggested that the Government simply had to pick which point on the Phillips curve it wanted the economy to be at and then introduce the appropriate policies.

However, in the 1970s there were high levels of inflation and high unemployment (called stagflation) which did not seem to fit with the original Phillips curve. The new situation was explained by an expectations augmented Phillips curve (Friedman). This model introduced short and long run Phillips curves and suggested that there was a short run trade off between inflation and unemployment but no long run trade off.

Expectations augmented Phillips curve

Each short run curve is constructed based on a level of expected inflation.

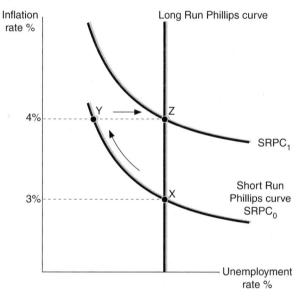

Imagine that the economy is at equilibrium at X. Employees expect inflation to be 3% and it is 3%; the economy is in long run equilibrium; unemployment is at the natural rate. Then an increase in aggregate demand pulls up inflation to 4%. Workers still expect 3% and are often locked into contracts for at least a year. This means in real terms employees are cheaper (they are getting paid 3% but prices are increasing at 4%), and so firms demand more labour. This excess demand for labour gradually pulls up money wages, e.g. to 3.5% and more workers accept jobs because they think they are better off

(note: in real terms they are actually worse off because inflation is 4%). Unemployment falls to Y. Over time, however, employees learn that inflation is 4% and bargain for more pay. Prices and wages will once again grow together at 4%; workers are no longer cheap in real terms and so the economy returns to full employment at Z.

Everyone now expects 4%, but if the Government uses expansionist policies which result in 5% inflation, the workers can once again be caught out. They will become relatively cheap because they are paid, say, 4.5% until they realise prices are growing at 5%.

To keep fooling the workers in future, the Government will have to bring about bigger jumps in inflation so employees can never predict what inflation will be next year. This model suggests that in the short run unemployment can be kept below full employment by fooling the employees, but it may require ever accelerating increases in inflation to do it. This assumes employees have 'adaptive expectations' and base their view of future inflation rates on what has happened in the past. Provided the Government keeps increasing inflation by accelerating rates, employees can be fooled.

In the long run there appears to be no trade off between inflation and unemployment; the economy returns to its long run equilibrium. Once employees realise what inflation is and increase their money wages accordingly, the real wage returns to the long run equilibrium and the economy is at full employment.

The short run trade off occurs because of 'money illusion' - employees focus on their money wages and not their real wages, e.g. when money wages rise, more people accept jobs in the short run even though real wages may not have increased; when workers realise what has happened to prices and demand higher nominal wages, the real wage is restored to long run equilibrium.

Rational expectations: people do not form expectations of future inflation based on the past, i.e. they do not have adaptive expectations - they look ahead and make an estimate based on all the information they have available at that moment, i.e. they are rational.

For example, if workers think the Government will reduce inflation in the future, they will cut their wage demands relatively quickly. This means the economy can adjust to the long run equilibrium fairly quickly and any short run Phillips curve is very short

run indeed. In its extreme version, rational expectations mean that workers cannot be fooled at all (i.e. there is no money illusion) and the Government cannot reduce unemployment below the natural rate even in the short run.

Aggregate demand and supply

This aggregate demand schedule shows the total level of planned expenditure on final goods and services at different prices, i.e. it shows the relationship between price and real national output.

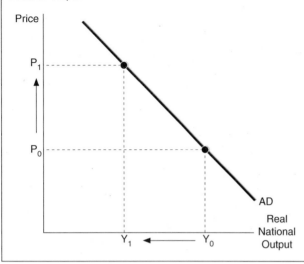

Shifts in the aggregate demand

caused by a change in factors other than price. An outward shift could be caused by:
- an increase in consumer or business confidence
- expansionist fiscal or monetary policy, e.g. lower tax rates, higher Government spending, higher exports, lower rates of interest, less spending on imports

Why does aggregate demand slope downwards?
- interest rates effect - with higher prices in the economy, nominal interest rates tend to increase. This reduces demand for goods which are sensitive to interest rates such as TVs, cars, or houses, which are usually bought on credit or with a loan.
- wealth effect - higher prices reduce the purchasing power of any cash balances. Individuals, therefore, tend to spend less.
- purchase of foreign goods and services - if UK prices increase, consumers and firms tend to switch to imports which are relatively cheaper. Also there will be less demand for UK goods from overseas.

Aggregate supply

Aggregate supply shows the level of real income (and output) in relation to the price.

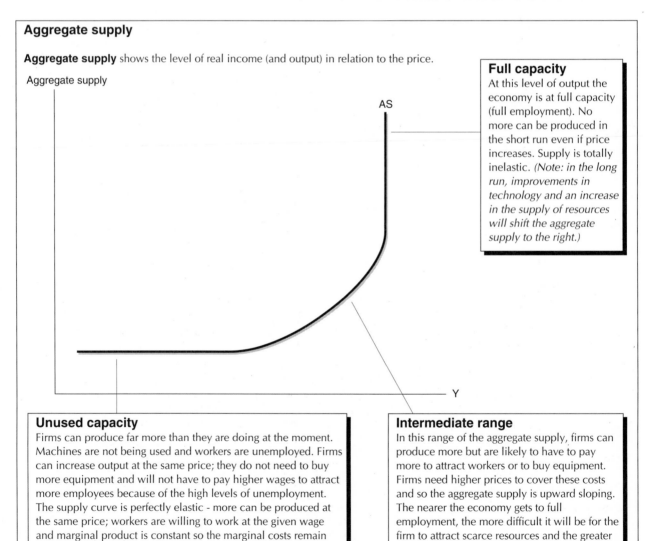

Full capacity
At this level of output the economy is at full capacity (full employment). No more can be produced in the short run even if price increases. Supply is totally inelastic. *(Note: in the long run, improvements in technology and an increase in the supply of resources will shift the aggregate supply to the right.)*

Unused capacity
Firms can produce far more than they are doing at the moment. Machines are not being used and workers are unemployed. Firms can increase output at the same price; they do not need to buy more equipment and will not have to pay higher wages to attract more employees because of the high levels of unemployment. The supply curve is perfectly elastic - more can be produced at the same price; workers are willing to work at the given wage and marginal product is constant so the marginal costs remain constant. An increase in aggregate demand increases real output and not prices below full employment as there is spare capacity in the economy.

Intermediate range
In this range of the aggregate supply, firms can produce more but are likely to have to pay more to attract workers or to buy equipment. Firms need higher prices to cover these costs and so the aggregate supply is upward sloping. The nearer the economy gets to full employment, the more difficult it will be for the firm to attract scarce resources and the greater the increase in costs (and therefore price) for each increase in output, i.e. the aggregate supply gets steeper (or more inelastic).

Aggregate demand and supply continued

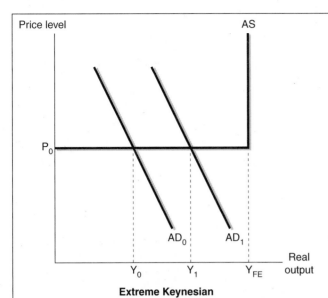

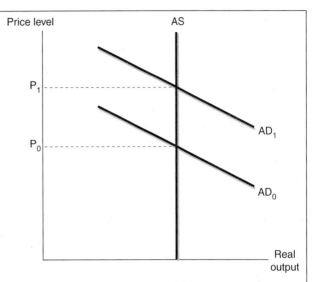

Extreme Keynesian
Up to full employment aggregate supply is horizontal, perfectly elastic. An increase in aggregate demand increases output and *not* prices. Only when full employment is reached will prices increase. The Government should control aggregate demand to ensure equilibrium occurs at full employment.

Extreme monetarist
(new classical)
Aggregate supply is vertical - any increase in aggregate demand increases the price level but *not* output and employment. To increase output and employment supply side policies are needed to shift aggregate supply to the right.

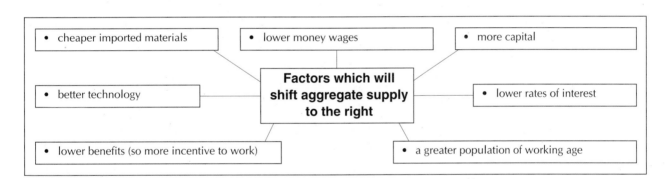

- cheaper imported materials
- lower money wages
- more capital
- better technology
- lower rates of interest

Factors which will shift aggregate supply to the right

- lower benefits (so more incentive to work)
- a greater population of working age

Supply side policies
Focus on increasing aggregate supply using microeconomic policies to improve the performance of markets, workers, and firms.
Policies include
- reducing Government spending - this will mean less money has to be borrowed by the Government and so more is available for the private sector

- cutting taxes so there is more incentive to work, e.g. cut the replacement ratio (this is the ratio of disposable income when unemployed, to disposable income when at work)
- reducing trade union power to increase the flexibility in the labour market

- cutting benefits so there is more incentive to work
- deregulating and privatising to increase competition
- making it easier for firms to set up; provide advice
- encouraging an entrepreneur culture

Supply side and taxation
Keynesians focus on the macro effects of changes in taxation and Government spending, e.g. a tax cut may increase aggregate demand. Supply side economics focuses on the micro effects, e.g. the effect of a tax cut on the incentive to invest or work.

Laffer curve
Higher tax rates will eventually lead to a decline in taxation revenue. The higher tax rates act as a disincentive for firms and employees - although the rate is higher, less people are working and so the revenue is lower. In this case, tax cuts can lead to more revenue for the Government (as more people want to work and firms want to expand).

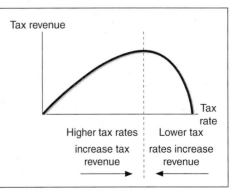

Aggregate demand and supply continued

From short run aggregate supply (SRAS) to long run aggregate supply (LRAS)

Each short run aggregate supply is drawn for a given money wage. If money wages increase, firms will want to hire less and produce less at every price level. The short run aggregate supply shifts up. If costs fall, e.g. due a fall in money wages, the aggregate supply shifts down.

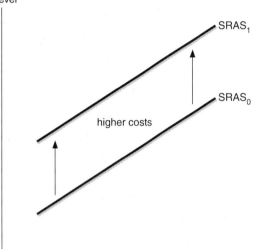

• an increase in aggregate demand

Long run equilibrium is at E; the economy is at full employment. An increase in aggregate demand pulls up the price level. The higher price reduces real wages, firms hire more and supply increases, as shown on the aggregate supply (point F). Firms are now producing beyond their normal capacity output, so there is excess demand for labour, pulling up money wages and shifting aggregate supply upwards (point G). If real wages return to the old level, equilibrium is restored at the full employment level; prices and money wages have both increased but the economy is back at full employment. The long run aggregate supply is vertical.

Keynesians think the move from short run to long run aggregate supply is slow, as money wages are slow to adjust. Monetarists think the adjustment is quick, as money wages are quick to adjust.

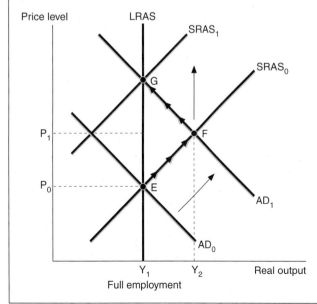

• a decrease in aggregate demand

Long run equilibrium is at E; the economy is at full employment. A decrease in aggregate demand leads to a fall in the price level and a new equilibrium at B. With the old money wages and a lower price, real wages have increased. Less is being produced and there is an excess supply of labour. The economy is below full employment. In the long run, money wages will fall, shifting aggregate supply downwards. With lower money wages and lower prices, the real wage returns to the long run equilibrium rate and the economy is back at full employment. Monetarists think this process is quick; Keynesians think money wages are slow to fall and so the economy can remain at B below full employment.

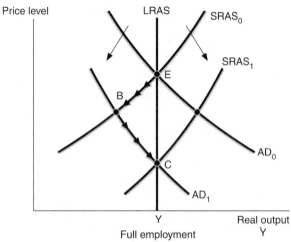

• the effect of an increase in costs

In the short run, an increase in costs shifts the aggregate supply upwards (to $SRAS_1$) as costs of production have risen. Price rises to P_1; output falls to Y_1. This illustrates 'stagflation', i.e. higher prices and lower output and employment. If the Government does nothing, then according to monetarist economists, the economy will return to the long run equilibrium - unemployment will put downward pressure on money wages, which reduces costs and the short run aggregate supply shifts back to SRASo. Keynesians argue this adjustment is likely to take a long time, because money wages are slow to fall. Alternatively, the Government could intervene by increasing the money supply and boosting demand, because output has fallen to Y_0. This reflationary action will shift aggregate demand outwards to AD_1; output returns to full employment level; and prices rise to P_2. The economy ends up back at full employment, with the natural rate of unemployment but higher prices.

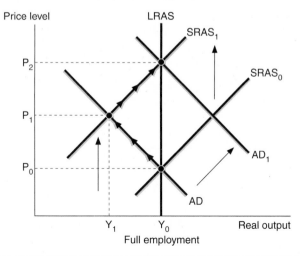

Keynesians and monetarists

Keynesians

1950s and 1960s Keynesians argued for demand management policies, i.e for the Government to control aggregate demand. If the economy grew too fast, the Government deflated; if it grew too slowly it reflated through fiscal policy. This led to a series of stop-go policies, e.g. deflate, reflate, deflate.

Keynesians believe that

- markets do not clear and are slow to adjust, e.g. the labour market. This means the economy can settle in equilibrium below full employment, so cyclical or 'involuntary unemployment' exists.
- the Government should intervene to stabilize the economy

- fiscal policy is more effective than monetary policy
- inflation is often caused by cost push factors

Extreme Keynesians believe

- markets do not clear and the economy will not move towards full employment. The Government must expand demand.

Monetarists

In the 1970s the UK experienced stagflation (high inflation and high unemployment). Existing theories struggled to explain it; monetarism grew in appeal.

Monetarism is based on the quantity theory of money, $MV = PY$. V and Y are assumed constant so prices are directly related to the money supply.

Monetarists believe

- that inflation is due to the money supply growing faster than output growth. Reducing the rate of growth of the money supply will lead to less inflation without more unemployment (in the long run) (see expectations augmented Phillips curve)
- prices and wages change quite quickly, so the economy tends towards full employment

- inflation makes firms uncompetitive, discourages investment, and so governments must control inflation. To do this they must control the money supply. Apart from this, the Government should intervene very little.

Extreme monetarists are called the **new classical school** - they believe markets clear quickly and expectations adapt very quickly. Faster growth of the money supply will quickly lead to inflation; even in the short run the Phillips curve is vertical.

Moderate monetarists believe

- markets adjust fairly quickly. An increase in the money supply and therefore demand will lead to some fall in unemployment in the short run. Similarly, a sharp reduction in the money supply may cause unemployment in the short run.

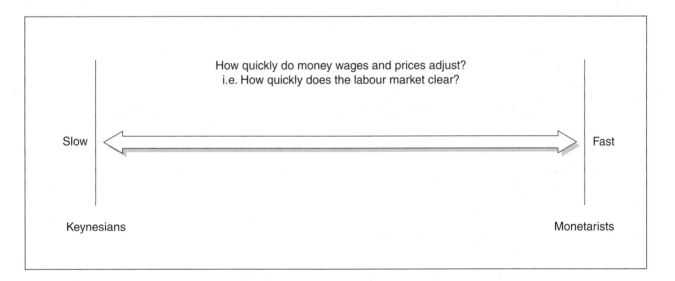

How quickly do money wages and prices adjust?
i.e. How quickly does the labour market clear?

Slow ⟵⟶ Fast

Keynesians   Monetarists

The labour market

The labour market is a key element of the economy and its ability to clear (i.e for supply to equal demand) is important. This depends on the flexibility of wages.
If aggregate demand falls and there is excess supply of labour, in a perfectly competitive world money wages will fall and the labour market will clear - the economy will remain at full employment.

BUT

- unions may fight against a fall in wages
- wages may take time to fall, e.g. they are often negotiated for a year in advance.
If wages do not fall, there will be unemployment for long periods of time and the economy can remain below full employment for long periods of time.

Monetarists believe that money wages and prices are flexible, and so the labour market clears - the economy is at or moving towards full employment.
Keynesians believe money wages and prices are not flexible, and so the labour market does not necessarily clear - the economy can be in equilibrium below full employment.

Exchange rates

The exchange rate is the price of one currency in terms of another. It is the external value of a currency (the internal value is what the currency can buy in its own country and depends on the price level). The UK exchange rate is called the 'value of the pound' or 'the value of sterling'.
In a floating exchange rate system, this price is determined by market forces of supply and demand.
In a fixed system the Government intervenes to maintain the external value of the currency.

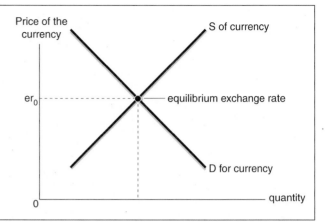

Changes in the exchange rate
- In a floating system, an increase in the exchange rate is an appreciation; a fall is a depreciation.
- In a fixed system, if the rate at which it is fixed is increased, this is a revaluation. If a lower rate is fixed it is a devaluation.

At any moment in time there are many exchange rates, e.g. the pound in terms of dollars, in terms of yen, in terms of francs and so on. The value of the pound can go up against some and down against others.

Trade weighted index: measures the value of sterling against a basket of currencies which are weighted according to their importance in UK trade.
Effective exchange rate: takes into account how much trade the country does with the other countries (and weights movements accordingly). It also considers the extent to which the country competes with these other countries internationally.
Real exchange rate: takes inflation into account. e.g. if the pound falls by 3% against the DM, but UK inflation is 3% higher than Germany's, the real exchange rate is unaltered.

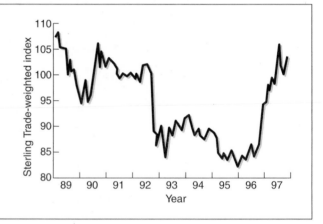

The demand for pounds (or sterling)
This refers to the desire to change other currencies into pounds in order to:
- spend on UK goods and services
- save in UK banks and other financial institutions (long term capital movements)
- speculate on the currency in the hope that the pound will become more valuable in the future (these are short term capital movements; called 'hot money')

The demand for pounds will increase if:
- UK goods and services are demanded more, e.g. the quality improves, foreign incomes increase or they are relatively cheaper, more tourism into the UK
- the UK interest rate increases, because there will be a greater desire to save in the UK to earn higher rates of return
- people think the value of the pound will rise in the future so they buy it now

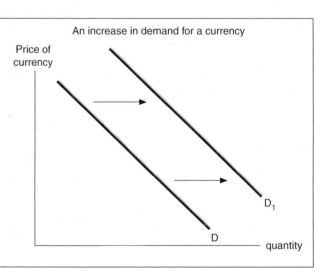

The elasticity of demand for pounds
If the pound falls, the price of UK goods or services in foreign currency also falls - demand for UK goods will increase. The extent of the increase and, therefore, the extent of the increase in the quantity demanded of pounds, depends on the price elasticity of demand for UK goods and services. The more elastic the demand for UK goods and services, the more elastic the demand for pounds.

Exchange rates continued

The supply of pounds (or sterling)

This refers to the desire to change pounds into other currencies in order to:

- buy overseas goods and services; travel abroad
- save in overseas financial institutions
- speculate on a foreign currency in the hope that it will increase in value

The slope of the supply of pounds

If the UK exchange rate falls, the price of imports in UK currency increases - this will reduce the amount of imports which are bought. If demand for imports is inelastic, the total amount spent on imports will increase and the supply of pounds is downward sloping.

If the demand for imports is elastic, then when their price rises in pounds (due to a fall in the value of the pound) the total amount spent on them falls. This means the supply of pounds is upward sloping.

The supply of pounds will increase if:

- overseas interest rates increase so saving abroad becomes more attractive
- overseas goods are demanded more, e.g. because they are better quality, UK incomes rise, or foreign goods are relatively cheaper; increased tourism abroad
- people think the pound will fall in the future so they sell it now

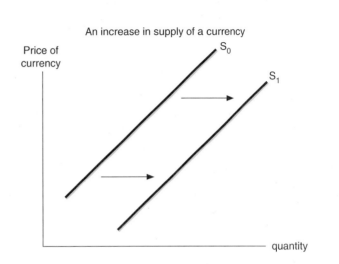

An increase in supply of a currency

Floating exchange rate system

The exchange rate is determined by demand and supply of the currency in the foreign exchange market. No Government intervention.

Advantages of a floating exchange rate system

- The exchange rate automatically adjusts so that supply equals demand - this can automatically eliminate balance of payments deficits or surpluses. If imports rise, for example, the supply of pounds increases, leading to a fall in the exchange rate. As the pound falls exports become more competitive and imports become less competitive which should eliminate the deficit.
- There is no need for the central bank to keep foreign reserves.
- The Government can pursue its own domestic policies, e.g. can adjust interest rates more easily.
- It prevents imported inflation - if one country has higher inflation, then, under a fixed exchange rates system, another country will import those via higher import prices.
- It possibly reduces speculation, because speculators might lose and so do not take the risk.

Disadvantages of a floating exchange rate system

- It causes instability which deters investment and trade (although business can hedge against exchange rate movements by buying or selling currency at some date in the future in the forward currency markets to reduce the risk).
- It can lead to inflation - if a country has inflation which makes its goods uncompetitive, this will lead to a fall in demand for its currency and a fall in the exchange rate. This makes its goods competitive again but makes imports more expensive, which in the long run will lead to more inflation (cost-push).
- Speculation on future movements can lead to major changes in the rate.
- Governments are not forced to control their economies, e.g. they do not have to ensure that domestic inflation is in line with other countries to ensure their firms are competitive (this is because the pound can float downwards).

Exchange rates continued

The Government and the exchange rate

The Government can influence the exchange rate by
- buying and selling currency
- changing the interest rate to influence capital inflows and outflows from the economy

To increase demand for the currency the Government can
- buy the currency
- raise interest rates to attract investors

Fixed exchange rate

The Government intervenes to maintain the exchange rate. If the price is about to fall, the Government increases demand by buying its own currency (using foreign currency reserves) or increasing interest rates. If the price is about to increase, the Government sells its own currency or lowers interest rates.

Advantages of fixed exchange rates
- They provide stability for firms and households - this encourages investment and trade.
- They act as a constraint on domestic inflation - if a country has higher inflation than its trading partners, it will become uncompetitive (the currency will not depreciate to offset the inflation). Firms have to control costs to compete.
- In theory they prevent speculation, as there is no point because the value of the exchange rate is fixed.

Disadvantages of fixed exchange rates
- A Government must have sufficient reserves to intervene to maintain the price of its currency.
- A country's firms may be uncompetitive if the exchange rate is fixed at too high a rate.
- The Government must make intervention a priority. This may mean it undertakes policies which damage the domestic economy, e.g to keep demand for pounds up in the exchange rate market, the Government might increase interest rates. The problem is that this leads to less demand within the country.

Managed exchange rate

Government intervenes on occasions to influence the price, but does not fix it.

Purchasing power parity (PPP)

The theory that in a floating system exchange rates adjust until a unit of currency can buy exactly the same amount of goods and services as a unit of another currency.

Exchange Rate Mechanism (ERM)

Each country agrees to stabilize its currency against a central rate, e.g. the UK joined at a central rate of 2.95DM. Each currency can fluctuate within a band around these currencies (usually 2.25% either way, although the pound was allowed to move 6% either way). The central bank must intervene to keep the currency within this band. If the central rate needs to be realigned, it can be if all members agree.

Why join the ERM?
- It may lead to less inflation - firms and workers realise that higher prices will not be offset by a lower exchange rate; this puts pressure on them to control costs and prices
- stability

UK experience in ERM

The rate at which the pound was fixed was too high, and this made UK firms uncompetitive. The Government had to intervene to keep the exchange rate within the set bands - it had to buy currency and increase interest rates. Higher interest rates made borrowing for firms and households more expensive within the UK. The effect of the ERM was to worsen the UK's recession. Speculators sold pounds putting even more pressure on the Government. The UK left the ERM in 1992.

Fiscal and monetary policy and exchange rate systems

Under a fixed exchange rate system, monetary policy becomes more difficult - any change in the interest rate is liable to lead to inflows or outflows of currency, and put pressure on the currency, e.g. the Government tries to control the money supply which leads to higher interest rates which encourage inflows on the capital account. These inflows increase the money supply again.

Fiscal policy is effective, e.g. the Government tries to deflate the economy through higher taxes and less spending. This reduces aggregate demand and spending on imports. Lower demand will also reduce demand for money and interest rates. Lower interest rates lead to capital outflow which reinforces the contractionary fiscal policy.

In a floating system monetary policy is more powerful

For example, an expansion of the money supply will reduce interest rates, which will boost spending within the economy. It will also lead to outflows of currency of the capital account. This will lead to a fall in the value of the currency, which will boost exports leading to a further increase in aggregate demand.

Alternatively, a tight (contractionary) monetary policy increases interest rates and reduces aggregate demand. Higher interest rates lead to capital inflows and an appreciation of the pound. This further reduces aggregate demand.

Fiscal policy is less effective, e.g. contractionary fiscal policy reduces income and demand for money. This reduces interest rates and leads to an outflow on the capital account. This in turn leads to a depreciation of the exchange rate which raises aggregate demand.

Balance of payments

Balance of payments

A record of a country's transactions with the rest of the world. It shows the country's payments and receipts from its trade. It consists of the capital and the current account.

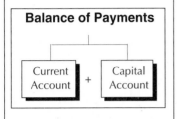

Balance of Payments

Current Account + Capital Account

Current account

- visible trade account - the difference between the export revenue and import spending on physical goods
- invisible trade account - measures the difference between export revenue and import spending on:

a) services, e.g. banking, insurance, and tourism
b) interest, profit, and dividends flowing in and out of the country
c) transfer payments, e.g. UK grants for overseas aid

Current account balance - balance of both visibles and invisibles.

Capital account

This records investments and financial flows. Movements in money capital by firms, households, and the Government, e.g. to invest in factories, in shares or payments to the EU.

If the Government intervenes in the exchange rate market to influence the value of the currency, there will be a third element in the balance of payments called 'official financing' - this shows the extent of intervention.

If, at the given exchange rate, there is excess demand for currency, i.e. there is greater demand for pounds than supply, the Government will have to sell pounds to keep the value constant. This is entered as a negative number under official financing on the balance of payments.

Current and capital account	SURPLUS	(POSITIVE)
Official financing	NEGATIVE	(the Government selling currency)
Total	0	

If at the given exchange rate there is an excess supply of pounds, the Government will have to buy pounds to keep the value constant. This is entered as a positive number under official financing.

Current and capital account	DEFICIT	(NEGATIVE)
Official financing	POSITIVE	(the Government buying currency)
Total	0	

If there is no official financing, the supply of currency will always equal the demand (i.e. outflows = inflows) and the balance of payments is 0. If there is a surplus on the current account, there is a deficit on the capital account and vice versa.

Balance of payments and floating exchange rates

In a free floating exchange rate system, the balance of payments will automatically balance. The exchange rate automatically changes until the supply of pounds equals the demand for pounds, i.e. the number of pounds leaving the country equals the number entering. This does not mean each element of the balance of payments balances, i.e the current account can be in deficit if the capital account is in surplus or vice versa

Balance of payments and fixed exchange rates

If the exchange rate is fixed above (er_0) the equilibrium rate there will be excess supply of currency, i.e more money wants to leave the country than come into it. This means that, excluding Government intervention, there is a balance of payments deficit.

If the price is fixed below the equilibrium rate (er_1) there will be excess demand for the currency, i.e more money wants to come into the country than leave it. This means that excluding Government intervention there is a balance of payments surplus.

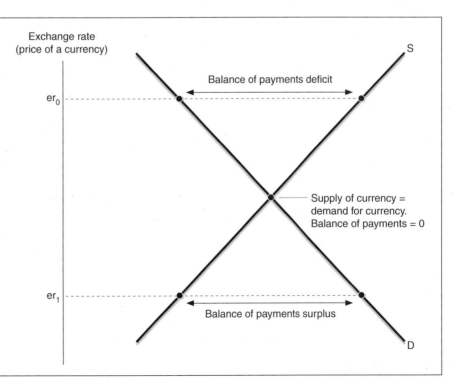

Balance of payments continued

Current account deficit
The UK is spending more on foreign goods and services than is being spent on UK goods and services. Money is leaving the country.

Problems of current account deficit
In the long run this could indicate problems with the competitiveness of a country's industries. Usually more of a problem in a fixed exchange rate system, compared to a floating rate. In a floating system the external value of currency falls, making exports competitive again. In a fixed system the deficit may be offset by inflows on the capital account or the Government will have to intervene to buy up excess currency (this cannot continue indefinitely as the country will run out of foreign currency reserves).

Policies to reduce a balance of payments deficit

- **Expenditure switching policies**
  These are attempts to make imports relatively expensive compared to exports, e.g.
  a) import controls such as tariffs
  b) bringing about a reduction in the exchange rate such as a devaluation

- **Expenditure reducing policies**
  The Government attempts to reduce spending throughout the economy, i.e deflate the economy. This is likely to reduce the amount spent on imports (although at the same time the amount spent on UK goods and services will also fall). To reduce spending, the Government could increase taxation rates, cut its own spending or increase interest rates.

Policy packages
It may be necessary to use a combination of policies, e.g. a depreciation will result in consumers switching from imports to exports.

However, if UK industry is at or near full capacity, it cannot produce enough and the result is inflation. Therefore, the Government might deflate the economy (expenditure reducing) to

provide capacity for a depreciation (expenditure switching). Expenditure reducing and expenditure switching policies are complementary, not substitutes.

The J curve effect

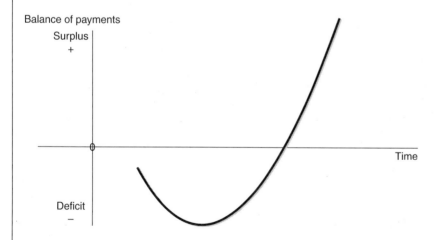

total amount spent on them will fall because demand is inelastic. Although the price of imports has risen, the total amount spent on them will rise because demand is inelastic. The overall result is that the balance of payments deficit actually worsens in the short run.

In the long run, consumers and firms find alternative cheaper suppliers in other countries and UK buyers switch to the cheaper foreign imports, i.e. the demand for imports and exports is price elastic. With the lower export prices spending on exports rises; with the higher import prices spending on imports rises and the balance of payments improves (see Marshall Lerner condition on next page).
In the very long run the balance of payments might worsen again. This is because the higher import prices can cause cost push inflation and make UK goods and services uncompetitive abroad. Many argue that a devaluation will <u>not</u> improve the balance of payments position over the very long term.

If the pound falls in value, this makes exports relatively cheap in foreign currencies and imports relatively expensive in pounds.

In the short run the demand for imports and demand for exports are likely to be inelastic. This is because consumers and firms have already got their sources of supply and may be reluctant to change. Although the price of exports falls in terms of foreign currency, the

Balance of payments continued

Marshall Lerner condition

When the pound falls, the price of exports in foreign currency falls and the quantity demanded will increase, leading to more pounds being spent (if demand is elastic). The extent of the increase depends on the price elasticity of demand for exports. Meanwhile, the fall in the pound increases the price of imports in pounds; the amount spent on imports will fall provided the demand for imports is elastic.

Overall the balance of payments will <u>improve</u> following a depreciation, provided

elasticity of demand for imports + elasticity of demand for exports >1

Income effect

If a depreciation leads to a fall in imports the country that produced these goods will suffer a fall in their income. If the UK exports to these countries, it may find its exports also suffer. Also, falling income levels may reduce pressure on prices in these countries so UK goods appear relatively expensive.

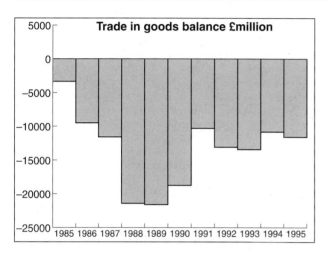

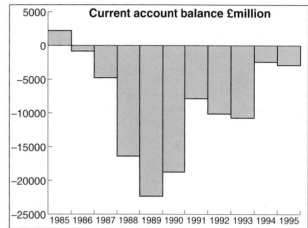

Absorption approach

examines the balance of payments from a Keynesian perspective, i.e the ability of the economy to absorb an increase in demand. For example, if the economy is at full employment, expenditure switching policies will lead to inflation. The economy must be deflated first to provide excess capacity so the economy can meet the higher demand from abroad.

Reducing a balance of payments surplus

- reflate to boost demand and so increase imports
- remove import controls
- revalue the currency

Problems of a balance of payments surplus

- one country's surplus is another's deficit - the country with the deficit may introduce protectionist measures
- Dutch disease effect - in the 1950s the Dutch discovered natural gas in the Netherlands; the gas was exported and generated large balance of payments surpluses, but the increase in demand for Dutch gas led to an increase in the exchange rate, which made Dutch companies uncompetitive. In the UK, North Sea oil brought about surpluses but led to appreciation of the pound, which damaged UK industry's competitiveness
- if the exchange rate is fixed, a balance of payments surplus will increase the domestic money supply (a surplus means there is excess demand for the currency so the authorities must sell currency). This increase in the money supply can lead to inflation

International trade

This is based on the principle of comparative advantage, which in turn is based on the concept of opportunity cost. If a country can produce good X with a lower opportunity cost than another country, it has a comparative advantage in the production of X. This means it sacrifices less of other goods to make one unit of X. By comparison, if its opportunity cost of producing good Y is higher than another country it has a comparative disadvantage.

Absolute advantage
A country has an absolute advantage in the production of a good if an equal quantity of resources can produce more of the good than another country. This does not mean it necessarily has a comparative advantage. Although it might be able to make more Xs than another country, it might also involve a greater sacrifice of other goods such as Y.

Free trade - no barriers to importing or exporting (i.e no protectionism), so trade occurs unhindered.

The benefits of free trade
Imagine resources are allocated between two goods X and Y in two countries A and B and the output is as follows:

	Good X	Good Y
Country A	1	4
Country B	2	3
TOTAL	**3**	**7**

The opportunity costs of production are as follows:

	Opportunity cost of 1X	Opportunity cost of 1Y
Country A	4Y	$\frac{1}{4}$X
Country B	$1\frac{1}{2}$Y	$\frac{2}{3}$X

If each country specializes in the production of the good in which it has comparative advantage, A will make Ys because the opportunity cost is $\frac{1}{4}$X rather than $\frac{2}{3}$X.
B will make X because the opportunity cost is $1\frac{1}{2}$Y rather than 4Y.

If all resources are now diverted into these goods, then, assuming constant returns to scale, the output will double (because there are twice as many resources in the production of these particular goods), i.e

	Good X	Good Y
Country A	0	8
Country B	4	0
TOTAL	**4**	**8**

Without trade the economies made 3Xs and 7Ys; with trade they make 4Xs and 8Ys, i.e there are more of both goods. Trade allows countries to benefit from more goods and services by specializing in goods and services where they have comparative advantage. International trade is always beneficial if there is a difference in the opportunity cost ratios between two countries. Through trade consumers can have a wider range of goods at a cheaper price than is possible if they do not trade.

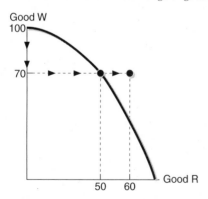

Trade enables countries to consume outside of their production possibility frontiers, e.g. without trade if the country gives up 30 units of W it achieves 50 units of R in return. With trade it may be able to export its 30W for 60R.

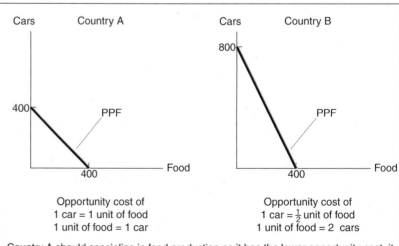

Opportunity cost of
1 car = 1 unit of food
1 unit of food = 1 car

Opportunity cost of
1 car = $\frac{1}{2}$ unit of food
1 unit of food = 2 cars

Country A should specialize in food production as it has the lower opportunity cost, it should import cars. Country B should export cars and import food

International trade continued

Further gains from trade
- economies of scale - by specializing, countries may increase their output and gain lower unit costs
- efficiency - the competition which arises from trade acts as an incentive to domestic firms to increase their competitiveness
- political, social, and cultural gains from bringing countries closer together

Limits to the benefits from free trade
- increasing costs of production - firms may suffer from diseconomies of scale
- transport costs may make it more expensive to trade, even if a country has comparative advantage

---

Terms of trade refer to the rate of exchange of one good for another between trading partners. Depends on the opportunity cost ratios, e.g. country A can make 1X for 4Y; country B can make 1X for 1.5Y.

Trade will occur if

$1.5Y > 1X < 4Y$ (e.g. $1X = 2Y$)

At this rate B sells Xs for more than it costs to make them; A buys them for less than it could produce them itself.

The terms of trade are measured by:

$\dfrac{\text{average export prices (index)}}{\text{average import prices (index)}} \times 100$

If export prices increase compared to import prices, the terms of trade improve (called a 'favourable' movement)

If export prices fall relative to import prices (e.g. do not increase as much) the terms of trade worsen (called an 'adverse' movement)

UK terms of trade

1985	1986	1987	1988	1989	1990	1991	1992	1993	1994	1995
101.9	96.1	96.7	98.6	98.8	100	100.2	101.4	103.5	102.2	98.9

Base year 1990

UK trade
- Most UK trade is with industrialised countries; increasingly within Europe.
- In recent years the balance of manufactured goods has been in deficit (due to the decline of manufacturing - deindustrialisation - and decline in competitiveness).
- from the 1970s (peaking in the mid 1980s) North Sea oil has made a positive contribution - without North Sea oil there would have been an even larger current account deficit.
- Most of the twentieth century there has been a deficit on the balance of visible trade and surplus on invisibles. The UK has lost competitive advantage in many manufacturing industries, but has comparative advantage in services, e.g. finance. Invisibles have also gained from net property income from abroad - the UK has invested heavily overseas and these investments are now paying dividends.

Protectionism: involves barriers to trade
- quotas - these place a limit on the number of foreign goods and services allowed into a country
- exchange controls - these place a limit on the amount of money which can be changed into foreign currency
- non tariff barriers, e.g. administrative procedures which make it difficult for foreign firms to sell their goods in the country (such as different safety standards)

Methods of protectionism

- tariffs (or import duties) - taxes placed on foreign goods to make them more expensive and encourage consumers to switch to domestic goods and services
- embargoes - when an embargo is placed on a good, no trade at all is allowed; often done for political reasons
- voluntary agreements, e.g. one government may pressurize another to reduce its exports (called a 'voluntary export restraint'), e.g. the Japanese agree to limit car exports to the UK

Reasons for protectionism
- infant industry argument - small firms need to be protected to give them time to expand and gain economies of scale, which will allow them to compete on an international basis
- dumping - to prevent foreign firms selling goods at a loss to destroy the domestic industry. If the foreign firms are going to sell at the low price indefinitely, the other country should welcome the cheap goods. If, however, it is simply a policy to destroy a domestic industry, then anti-dumping tariffs might be justified
- to raise revenue through tariffs
- to prevent overspecialization and diseconomies of scale
- to remove a balance of payments deficit (but this does not solve the underlying cause of the deficit)

International trade continued

Non economic reasons for protectionism

- strategic interests - some industries (such as defence and agriculture) may need to be kept in national hands for strategic reasons (e.g. in case of war)
- political reasons, e.g. a country may not want to trade with another because of political differences
- to prevent the import of harmful goods, e.g. a country may want to ban the import of certain literature or drugs
- way of life - a country may want to keep its existing way of life, e.g. protect farming
- protection against low wage economies. Some countries use protectionism to combat the low wages paid elsewhere. This is <u>not</u> an economic argument for protectionism. If one country has a comparative advantage because it pays low wages, the other country should welcome the cheaper goods and services and concentrate on producing items where it has a comparative advantage.

Effect of a tariff

Price

Domestic supply

Tax revenue for the Government

Welfare loss on units q_3q_2 the extra benefit to the consumer exceeded the old price. Now these units are not bought due to higher price

Inefficiency area, inefficient domestic producers can now supply due to tariff

P_1

World supply and tariff

tariff

P_0

World supply

Demand

Quantity

q_0 q_1 q_3 q_2

new level of imports

Transfer to domestic producers. Consumers pay more which goes to producers

original imports

Alternatives to protectionism

Even if some of the arguments for protectionism are valid, the same results can usually be achieved more efficiently. For example, the Government could subsidize domestic production - this would have the effect of making more goods and services available at a cheaper price rather than restricting consumer choice to fewer goods at a higher price. Politically this is less popular, since the subsidies may have to be financed out of higher taxes, and imposing a tariff on foreign producers looks more aggressive.

- **Free trade area:** free trade between member countries; members are allowed to charge whatever tariffs they wish against non member countries.
- **Customs union:** free trade between member countries; members must charge a common external tariff against non member countries.

Gains of customs unions

- internal economies of scale - firms operate in a larger market and may be able to increase output and sales and reduce the unit cost
- greater competition can improve efficiency
- the union as a whole can have more bargaining power and get better terms of trade

BUT consider
- the cost of administering the union
- the possibility of diseconomies of scale

International institutions

- International Monetary Fund
  Aim: to provide finance to maintain exchange rate stability - countries pay into the fund, which will lend to them when they need additional finance to support their currency, e.g. the UK in 1976. IMF loans are given with certain conditions, e.g. that the Government must control the growth of its money supply or cut its spending.
- The World Bank
  Funds development projects such as dams and roads, especially in the developing world.
  Interest is charged so the projects must pay their way.

- GATT (now the World Trade Organisation) General Agreement on Tariffs and Trade
  Set up in 1945. Member countries try to reduce the level of protectionism between them. Now called the World Trade Organisation. The first GATT meeting was in 1947. Since then there have been various 'rounds' of negotiations, such as the Tokyo round and the Uruguay round.

Developing economies

Types of economy:
- First World - highly developed and industrialized, e.g. Western Europe and USA
- Second World, e.g. Eastern Europe - living standards usually lower than First World, and higher proportion of the economy is involved in agriculture; less developed service sector
- Third World - developing economies, e.g. several countries in Africa, Latin America
  Some have developed quite fast e.g. Malaysia; others have yet to develop significantly

Problems of Less Developed Countries (LDCs)
- LDCs are often dependent on one or two commodities for export earnings, which can lead to instability. This causes problems because:
- **a)** these goods usually have price inelastic supply and demand - any shift in supply or demand can have major effects on price
- **b)** technological developments have reduced the need for some natural commodities produced by LDCs
- **c)** income elasticities for these products are usually low - as economies grow, demand for, e.g. foodstuffs, typically grows at a slower rate
- **d)** of increased supply - again technological developments have improved yields of these products, which shifts supply to the right and brings down the price, worsening terms of trade; a falling price of commodities means that these countries' exports buy less imports
- rapid population growth
- high interest repayments due to high levels of borrowing
- lack of appropriate technology
- some countries have high spending on defence

Policies to improve the LDC situation
- Import substitution - countries put tariffs onto foreign goods to protect their own industries. The problem is that protected industries may simply become inefficient. Often criticised as an 'inward looking strategy'
- more trade - this is an outward looking strategy; encourages foreign investment and seeks to export (e.g. Singapore and Hong Kong)

International commodity agreements
Attempts by member countries to control the supply and so the price of their commodities.

Developing economy: low real income per capita compared to, e.g. Western industrialized countries, USA, and Japan. Usually have a low life expectancy, low literacy, and a high agricultural sector. However, there is a wide variety of developing countries - some very poor, e.g. Ethiopia; others such as Korea, Taiwan, and Singapore have been very successful at raising living standards.

Main monetary indicator of the economic status of a country: GNP per capita
Non monetary indicators of the welfare of a country: life expectancy, adult literacy
The distribution of income and wealth must always be considered

What causes growth?
- natural resources - although many successful countries like Japan only have a few natural resources
- capital - both human and physical; countries which grow fast have usually invested in better education and nutrition.
- technology
- entrepreneurship

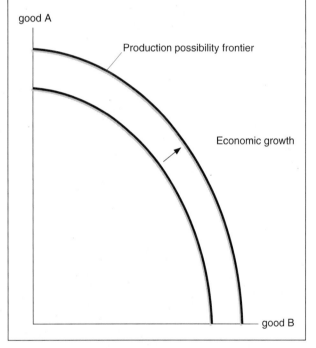

Aid
- often aid remains in the hands of a few and does not trickle down into the economy
- often focuses on the cities not the country as a whole
- may reduce the incentive for the country to develop its own industry - may lead to reliance on aid
- governments in aid-giving countries often want to cut it when they need to reduce their own deficits - LDCs cannot rely on it
- banks often charge high interest rates - debt repayments can become a major burden
- may be better to concentrate on opening markets to trade to allow LDCs the opportunity to export

Economic reason for aid
By helping developing countries develop, a country is creating markets to export to in the future.

Trickle down effect: the idea that the benefits of faster growth would work their way through the economy so that all groups benefited - in reality, e.g. in Brazil, some groups benefit but others do not gain so much.

Developing economies

- rapid population growth - if population grows at the same rate as income, the income per capita stays constant. If population growth exceeds the income growth, the income per person falls.

- human resources, e.g. if the workforce is untrained or poorly educated or in bad health, growth will be more difficult.

- poor natural resources, e.g. if a country has poor resources, growth can be more difficult. However, it also depends on how these resources are maintained and used

Barriers to growth for LDCs

- lack of an effective financial system - financial institutions enable firms to invest. If, however, people are reluctant to save or no effective bank system exists, there will not be enough savings to finance investment.

- cultural barriers, e.g. some people do not trust banks and so do not save

- poor use of resources, e.g. labour is unemployed or firms have no incentive to be efficient because of a lack of competition

- more investment in people, e.g. health care, better diets, education, training

- policies to encourage trade

- policies to encourage saving and investment

- policies to encourage productive use of land, e.g. fertilisers, equipment, irrigation systems

Policies to encourage growth in LDCs

- policies to encourage entrepreneurship

- improvements in appropriate technology

- policies to encourage development of infrastructure, e.g. roads, railways, dams

The European Union

The EU is a custom union, i.e free trade between member countries and common external tariffs with non members.
This brings about:
- trade creation - i.e. new trade is created between member countries which can benefit from free trade. Trade creation occurs when trade is shifted from a high cost producer to a low cost producer

- trade diversion - trade which would have occurred with countries outside the Union is diverted to the Union because the tariff makes it too expensive. Trade diversion occurs when trade is diverted from a low cost producer outside the Union to a higher cost producer within the Union.

1992 The Single Market
Freedom of movement of capital, people, and goods. Standards have been harmonized, limits on the movement of money have been removed, and qualifications of member countries have become accepted within the Union.

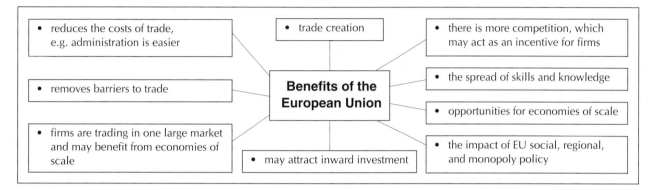

- reduces the costs of trade, e.g. administration is easier
- removes barriers to trade
- firms are trading in one large market and may benefit from economies of scale
- trade creation

Benefits of the European Union

- there is more competition, which may act as an incentive for firms
- the spread of skills and knowledge
- opportunities for economies of scale
- the impact of EU social, regional, and monopoly policy
- may attract inward investment

Revenue of the EU: comes from agricultural levies and tariffs on imports, from member governments, and from VAT

Spending of the EU: the majority is used on the Common Agricultural Policy. Other spending includes Structural Funds to help depressed areas, industry, and social policy.

EU institutions
- European Commission
  Commissioners are appointed by member countries to administer policies and propose policies.
- European Council of Ministers - senior ministers from each country; different ministers for different committees
- European Parliament - Members of the European Parliament are elected in constituencies in each country

- domestic firms may suffer from competition
- impact of EU policy e.g social policy

Disadvantages of the European Union

- European monopolies may develop
- trade diversion
- have to pay contributions into EU budget

Social Charter
Covers workers' rights in areas such as:
- freedom of movement
- working conditions
- minimum employment age
- health and safety
- consultation and participation at work

Full monetary union: a single currency
To be allowed to be part of monetary union, countries have to meet set criteria which were established by the Maastricht Treaty (1993):
- inflation - no more than 1.5% above the inflation of the 3 countries in the EU with the lowest inflation
- interest rates - on long term bonds no more than 2% above the average of the 3 countries with the lowest interest rates
- budget deficit - no more than 3% of GDP at market prices
- national debt - no more than 60% of GDP at market prices
- exchange rates - their currency should have been within normal bands for at least two years with no realignments or excessive intervention

EMU (European monetary union)
Established 1979. It attempted to create greater exchange rate stability between member countries of the European Union. Involves:
- ECU - members currencies are denominated in European currency units (ECUs). The ECU is a weighted average of member currencies. The ECU is used for settling debts between various central banks.
- EMI (European Monetary Institute) - member countries deposit some of their dollar and gold reserves. In return the EMI provides credit facilities to support countries in exchange rate difficulties
- Exchange Rate Mechanism - a combination of fixed and floating exchange rates. Member countries are allowed to fluctuate against each other within a specific band.

In the late 1990s, some member countries moved towards full monetary union, i.e. a single currency called the 'euro'.

EMU – single currency
benefits
- no cost of converting currency, i.e. no transaction costs with currency
- removes uncertainty about exchange rates
- forces countries to control inflation (or they become uncompetitive)

but
- some regions (countries) may gain more than others
- some commentators worry about political effects of loss of control over a country's currency

Growth and economic cycles

- resources - the more resources that a country has, and the more effectively it uses its natural resources, the more it can grow

- investment in people - the more that countries invest now, the more likely it is that they will grow in the future. Better training and better research, for example, may lead to future growth

Growth
The rate of growth of an economy depends on:

- technology - as technology improves, countries can use their existing resources more productively

- capital goods - investment in capital goods increases productivity and leads to future growth

- savings - saving enables investment by providing the funds for firms to invest

To help growth
- promote saving, e.g. provide incentives for households to save
- promote research and development
- promote education, e.g. provide funds for education, ensure qualifications are relevant to industry
- promote mobility of factors of production between industries
- promote supply side policies, e.g. remove barriers to labour market flexibility, cut taxes to increase incentives, improve the amount and quality of information available

Arguments against growth
- causes external costs, e.g. pollution
- may reduce quality of life, e.g. more income growth may involve less leisure time, pollution, movement away from the countryside towards the towns

The 'zero growth proposal' argues that because of the external cost of growth, governments should aim for 0 growth.

Economic cycles (also called business or trade cycles)

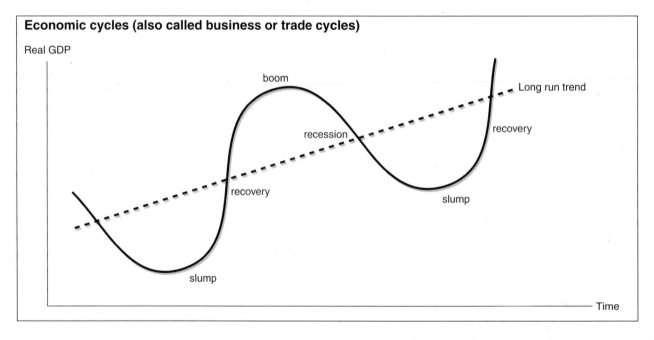

Term	Characteristics
Slump or depression	heavy unemployment, low levels of aggregate demand
Recovery	economy picks up; demand increasing; firms begin to invest
Boom	more confidence in the economy, investment high but beginning to be shortages of supply (e.g. of labour)
Recession	downswing of the economy; falling demand and rising stocks of unsold goods; some firms will close and unemployment will rise

Growth and economic cycles

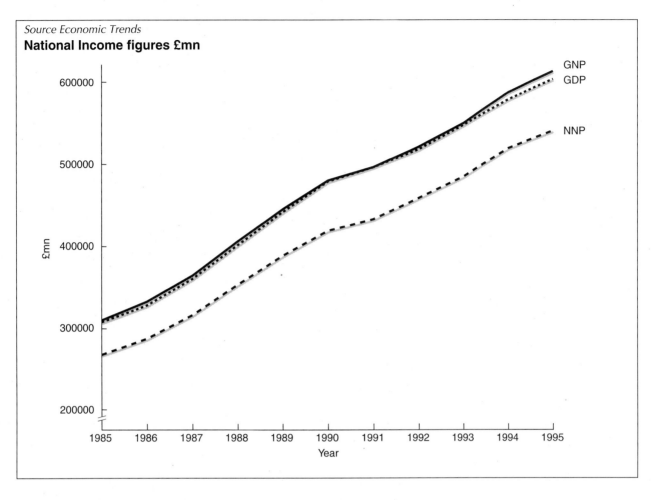

Source Economic Trends
National Income figures £mn

Reasons for the economic cycle:

- Political - in the run up to an election, the Government will want the economy to grow, and is likely to increase the level of demand. This causes growth and falling levels of unemployment. Post election, the Government may face demand pull inflation due to there being too much demand in the economy and may have to deflate the economy.

- Multiplier accelerator model - the multiplier and accelerator can work together to create booms and slumps.

For example, an increase in injections can set off the multiplier, which leads to an increase in output. To produce this output, firms increase their level of net investment which sets off the multiplier. At some point the economy begins to reach full capacity and output cannot easily be increased. Output may rise but by less than before - this causes a fall in the level of net investment (accelerator) and so a downward multiplier. However, there is a limit to how much investment will fall, i.e. a floor to the recession - some firms will always be investing, e.g. to replace equipment.

- Inventory cycle - firms are often slow to adjust to changes in the level of economic activity. When they do change, their decisions can often exaggerate the economic cycle. For example, if demand falls, firms may be reluctant to cut output in the short run until they are convinced the fall in demand will last. In the short run they build up stocks because they continue producing at the old level, even though demand has fallen. At some point firms realise that demand has fallen and cut back on output. Given that they have built up stocks, firms will cut output below the level of demand. This causes a further fall in aggregate demand, i.e it worsens the slump.

Similarly, when demand picks up, firms use up stocks in the short run. In the long run, firms will expand their capacity, invest and produce more. Given that they have used up their stocks, they will increase output to a level above demand, so they can rebuild them. This gives an additional boost to the boom.

Indicators of changes in the level of economic activity:

- leading indicators - these give an indication that a boom or slump *might* happen, e.g. surveys of business confidence, new house purchases

- coincident indicators - these show when a boom or slump *is* happening, e.g. the level of sales
- lagging indicators - these *follow* the boom or slump, e.g. unemployment (firms are reluctant to make people redundant until they are sure that the economy is in a recession; similarly they are slow to hire people until they know the economy is recovering)

INDEX